Loop -d-Loop *Lace*

MORE THAN 30
NOVEL LACE DESIGNS
FOR KNITTERS

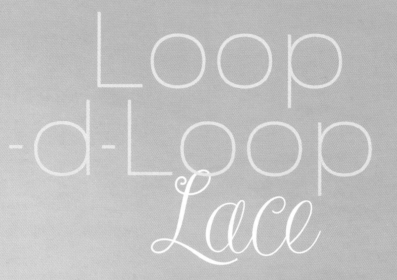

Loop -d-Loop *Lace*

MORE THAN 30 NOVEL LACE DESIGNS FOR KNITTERS

Teva Durham

PHOTOGRAPHS BY
ADRIAN BUCKMASTER

STC CRAFT | A MELANIE FALICK BOOK

STEWART, TABORI & CHANG
NEW YORK

To O.G.D. and L.G.D., my children in body and spirit;
and to my children in craft, wherever they may be.

Published in 2011 by Stewart, Tabori & Chang
An imprint of ABRAMS.

Edited by Liana Allday

Book Design: Anna Christian
Production Manager: Tina Cameron

Text copyright © 2011 by Teva Durham
Photographs copyright © 2011 by Adrian Buckmaster

Library of Congress Cataloging-in-Publication Data:
Durham, Teva.
 Loop-d-loop lace / by Teva Durham ; photography by Adrian Buckmaster.
    p. cm.
 ISBN 978-1-58479-834-7 (alk. paper)
1. Knitted lace—Patterns. I. Title.
 TT805.K54D87 2011
 746.2'26—dc22
                                              2010037765

The text of this book was composed in Gotham and Tribute.

Printed and bound in China
10 9 8 7 6 5 4 3 2 1

THE ART OF BOOKS SINCE 1949

115 West 18th Street
New York, NY 10011
www.abramsbooks.com

CONTENTS

INTRODUCTION

I HAD MY FIRST TRY AT KNITTED LACE UNDER THE TUTELAGE OF A MASTER.
A five-minute session, that is, via long-distance phone call. There I was, a
new hire in the offices of *Vogue Knitting,* which in those days was part of
Butterick. In my hands were short bamboo needles, size 7, with a half-
inch of flimsy, holey garter stitch in gray laceweight Icelandic wool. The
phone balanced in the crook of my neck, I was explaining to Meg Swansen
that I was assigned to knit a swatch of one of her lace patterns, which
would be photographed and included in the magazine to promote her new
yarn. On my desk lay a smudgy printout of a traditional shawl edge Meg
had faxed from Wisconsin. I considered myself a skilled knitter, but I had
never done an edging with yarnovers every row. This stitch pattern was to
have an undulating zigzag edge, but none of my 5-row efforts at following
the pattern repeat were looking much like the description (there was no
image, nor chart, on the page). My heart was racing. The photographer
was going to be ready for the shot in twenty minutes, yet there seemed to
be a few extra stitches on that sixth row.

Meg talked me through each pattern row and soon a rippling ribbon
of lace with a dainty yet rustic texture extended from the needles. Before
calling Meg, my initial faltering swatch attempts had not read as lace. The
yarnovers had been caught and twisted over the decrease, so I wasn't able
to observe the order in which they fell. I had to allow space for each loop
on the needle, relax, and be led one row at a time. Once I began to work the
stitches in the correct order, I marveled at the pretty strip I created: the
wandering, sheer lanes of interlaced stranding and artful solid wedges
that pointed first right, then took a sharp left. This knitterly engineering
feat fascinated me. I remember admiring the crisscrossing lane of yarnovers, and saying to myself, "All of this is inaccessible mojo to me now, but
one day . . . one day I will be able to draw upon this."

Every time I come across that standard reference to Meg Swansen on
the technical difference between knitted lace and lace knitting (which is
very often as she is a go-to source on the subject), I am reminded of our
first interaction. So here I am more than a decade later, writing the introduction to my very own lace book—which, by the way, contains both
knitted lace (lace worked on every row, says Meg) and lace knitting (with
a plain row in between).

When knitted lace was suggested as the theme of my third book, I was ready (though somewhat terrified) to take on the time-honored tradition and make my mark on it. With this book, I hope to inspire knitters who are just beginning to journey into lace as well as to prompt budding designers, very much like I once was, to explore ways to adapt the tradition of lace to their personal style. With that in mind, I've presented projects of the simplest lace stitches as well as more intricate ones, and I've made an effort to manipulate and utilize lace in unexpected ways. I have divided the book into five sections—Mesh, Eyelets, Samplers, Leaves, and Doilies—according to the family of stitches or the textiles that were the inspirational sources for the projects. The progression and scope of individual chapters, organized loosely from easiest to more complex projects, are intended to foster familiarity with lace genres and mastery of lace techniques. Each chapter's gallery of images, presented separately from its patterns, is accompanied by commentary on the evolution of the design. My aim was to survey the many different types of lace created throughout history while at the same time producing a collection of knits that felt authentic to my design sensibility.

Over the years, as I earned my designing chops, I merely dabbled in lace. Shortly after my *Vogue Knitting* stint I hit upon my own style and in 2000 I launched my line, Loop-d-Loop. My designs filled a niche for the new wave of knitters. I focused on quicker knits with an urban edge and an artisan look. While lace was not my forte or particular passion, some of my most successful designs featured lace stitchwork utilized in novel ways, such as the Lace Leaf Pullover from my first book, *Loop-d-Loop*, in which isolated pairs of leaves extend directionally from the collar and hem. Around the time *Loop-d-Loop* was published, I started to notice—both on the Internet and at knitting conferences—the growing number of lace enthusiasts showing their skillfully done, delicate, and intricate lace shawls. For many knitters, mastering the techniques to make such shawls is a rite of passage. And as I worked on this book, I was excited to see an abundance of sheer and lacy knit garments become fashionable at retail shops, worn casually over tanks and camisoles. While designing the pieces for this book, I set out to create a delectable fusion of lace that would call out to be knitted by today's lace knitters—those seeking something traditional and those seeking something a bit quirky.

I began my research by mining stitch dictionaries to find lace patterns that spoke to me. The visual library provided by stitch dictionaries was invaluable and the swatching process fascinating, especially when beginning with a stitch pattern shown only in a black and white photo (or in some cases a lithograph). In most cases, I swatched with a series of yarns and needle sizes to enhance specific qualities I discerned in the stitchwork. The stitch treasuries of Barbara G. Walker were particularly helpful as she often notes stitches that are associated with one another and shows them juxtaposed or stacked in the same swatch to illustrate differences. These associations inspired several patterns in this book. For instance, I utilized Walker's lesson on an every-row versus an every-other-row chevron for the hem of the Chevron Eyelet Skirt on page 50 as I loved the syncopation of the two chevron styles. I gravitated toward patterns with an Art Deco feel and sought out ones that I had not seen overly published. And I found such variety in the leaf patterns I encountered that I gave them their own chapter.

My favorite part of the process was researching the history of lace, and the historical aspect did factor into my selection of particular stitch patterns and silhouettes. For me, the very idea of lace evokes images from art history, such as the sixteenth-century portrait of Sir Walter Raleigh in his lace ruff. In the Renaissance, lace was created with bobbins and needles and was an extravagantly expensive commodity reserved for the ruling class. Knitted and crocheted lace was developed in imitation of this bobbin and needle lace and was a way for the less privileged to produce lacy trimmings and accessories at home. The popular taste for lace grew in Victorian times when lace abounded on linens and in fashions. As early as the 1830s, factories producing perforated paper lace doilies and Valentine's Day cards flourished. The sociological associations of lace and its noble/humble beginnings are fascinating to me. Lace, more so than any other textile, connotes innocence (christening gowns and wedding veils) and also seduction (Moulin Rouge-styled petticoats). I tried to hit the right notes with my designs, to reference and rework historical lace in fresh and pretty ways. I aimed for a particular mix of minimal and modern, with just a drop of sentimentality and drama, and an underlying lush element bestowed by hints of historic costume and boudoir frills. And with all the historical images to draw from, I couldn't resist designing a Palm Leaf Wrap that can be worn around the neck like a ruff (page 152), and the Lace Puff Bloomers (page 58), or reinventing a nineteenth-century classic, like the Hug-Me-Tight Cardigan (page 148).

In designing the garments in this book, I made other specific stops along the timeline of hand-knitting. For instance, the Shetland Island knitters of the mid-nineteenth century play an important role in many of

my designs. It seems to me that the Shetland shawls of that era mark the point when knitted lace gained a presence as a medium apart from other forms of lace. As I researched Shetland shawls, I mused on how to honor the art form while bringing it into the twenty-first century. In one interpretation, I tipped this traditional shawl on its side and turned it into one of my favorite garments: the Shetland Shawl Dress (at left and on page 87). For an easier project, I created the Shetland Twins Capelet (page 82), a contemporary design with an isolated Shetland lozenge pattern.

As lace became more and more accessible to the growing middle classes in the twentieth century, there was a taint to it. The term "lace curtain Irish," which I remember being used derogatorily for one side of my family, referred to the upwardly mobile working class who, aspiring to be a part of the elite, might hang such frilly, starched curtains in the window. After World War I, fashion turned away from the extravagance and fussiness of the Belle Epoque to a more sleek and modern aesthetic. But homemakers and hobbyists continued to enjoy magazines that featured craft patterns and during the 1930s a craze for intricate knitted doilies called *Kunststricken* (art knitting) began. The extraordinary doilies of Herbert Niebling and Marianne Kinzel, the masters of this style, were an important source of inspiration for this book. Many contemporary knitters are rediscovering *Kunststricken*, but for the most part they are working the doilies as whole tablecloths or circular shawls. While these are beautiful in their original form, they do not exactly fit with contemporary décor or fashion. In Chapter 5 I have manipulated doilies in novel ways in order to show how adaptable they are. I especially enjoyed playing with the wedge-like shape of isolated repeats. For instance, a doily motif became the halter triangles for the bust of the Thistle Bodice (page 136), and a small area of another doily with a sunray motif creates the Sunflower Satchel (page 132).

Most importantly, I think that all of these lace genres throughout history resonate with modern knitters and are exciting for contemporary designers to explore. A sense of whimsy and frivolity seems to go along with this frilly textile form. But at the same time, there is a seriousness to the simple beauty of the openwork stitches. Fortunately, the pastime of knitting has not faded away and knitters have never lost their love for the sheer art of working these astounding stitches.

Teva

MESH

Faggoting and Simple Openwork

THE PROJECTS IN THIS CHAPTER FEATURE OPENWORK FABRIC MADE BY pairing a decrease and a yarnover—the simplest players in the lace repertoire—across a row. These mesh stitch patterns have a charming, rustic appeal and are a great place for a beginning lace knitter to start. Most of these patterns are accomplished in one- or two-row repeats—the trick is to be mindful of the pattern's simple sequence (whether the yarnover comes before or after the decrease), and to keep an eye on the yarnover from the previous row to make sure it appears in the correct place when worked into the decrease. Once you relax and commit the sequence to memory, you get into a rhythm that has a lovely symmetry with the upswing of the yarnover and the underswing of the decrease.

Faggoting is a general term for many of these mesh stitches. Its name stems from the classic interlacing embroidery stitch often used on bed and table linens to decoratively join the fabrics' edges. These embroidery stitches were thought to resemble a spindly bundle of sticks tied together for firewood, which the British call a faggot. Trellis is another well-known stitch in this family, possessing a strong diagonal line, much like a garden trellis, and straighter openwork rungs. The diagonal lines can be manipulated to climb in either direction. All of the simple mesh variations presented here have individual character. Notice the solid columns formed by the decreases. Do they run in straight vertical lines or on the bias? Do they wiggle back and forth like rickrack trim? In the open yarnover columns, do the strands lie flat like ladder rungs, or do they cross each other from side to side to form x's? These mesh stitches are the building blocks of much more complex lace patterns. Once you familiarize yourself with the appearance of openwork stitch combinations, you will begin to recognize mesh in more complicated patterns where they become backgrounds and accents to solid shapes.

In this chapter, I use an array of mesh as allover patterns or in combination with Stockinette stitch to create a variety of garments and accessories. I've used some clever techniques and simplified construction to account for garment shaping within these stitch patterns, and I have worked the projects in several different fiber weights and textures, including drapey silk, dry linen, and even waxy leather cord, in order to show the variety of textural possibilities.

trellis beret and capelet

For this poofy beret and matching capelet, I've used Diagonal Trellis stitch, which is particularly easy to create when worked circularly—just yarnover then knit two together for every stitch of every round. While the braid-like columns of decreases travel toward the right, the open columns of stranded yarn lie flat and straight, resembling dropped stitches. The diagonal columns are quite dramatic at a chunky gauge, and, like paper lanterns children make in school, the open structure collapses and expands.

To shape the hat and capelet here, I developed a method that brings in new columns without interrupting the established pattern by working an extra set of stitches into the strand between each column. For an even simpler hat or capelet, you could work a circular knit tube in this pattern (cast on enough for the widest measure-ment), work without shaping to the desired length, then use a drawstring to gather it up at the top. For a fancier look, you could work an edging strip (such as Snail Shell on page 80) and sew it along the bottom of the capelet. Or try varying the stitch pattern by working plain knit stitches in between the Trellis (you could do this by following the chart for the socks on page 34).

>> See pattern on page 24.

butterfly lace tunic dress

On this dress, which can go from casual to party worthy, I've used an openwork stitch pattern, variably called Butterfly or Honeycomb. The stitch is basically a ladder stitch of squiggly columns, an effect caused by paired decreases in alternating directions that run along the yarnover "rungs," and are arranged in a half-drop design. The name comes from the lines that flutter inward and outward forming a mesh of cells. To bring out the botanical quality of the stitch, I chose a linen blend yarn—a ribbon wrapped with a metallic filament—which has a dry hand and subtle metallic shimmer.

>> See pattern on page 26.

portcullis jacket

Portcullis, a grilled meshwork in aligned columns, is a stitch found in Barbara Walker's *Second Treasury of Knitting Patterns*. This stitch adds structure as well as a romantic name to the military-style jacket here. A portcullis is a gate that can be lowered to fortify the entrance of a medieval castle, often with elaborate metalwork. In London there is a magnificent contemporary portcullis-inspired building across from Big Ben that houses Parliament and the Westminster tube station.

While the stitch pattern looks like an intricate and dimensional lacy ribbing, it is actually a simple 2-row pattern repeat—one row of yarnovers and decreases and one plain purled wrong-side row. The jacket is fitted but I've simplified the shaping by changing needle size to draw in the waist. You have the option of forming real or mock pockets with handsome buttoned flaps.

>> See pattern on page 28.

old shale belt

In this belt, I've used a very common lace pattern, Old Shale, in an unusual way: it uses one isolated repeat for the strip of the belt and it is worked in leather cord. Old Shale is the next logical progression toward lace after faggoting stitches. Rather than repeated pairs as in faggoting stitches, there is a grouping of yarnovers between plain stitches, and a separate grouping of decreases. Known in several variations and sometimes called Feather and Fan, Old Shale is thought to be original to Shetland Island and named for the ripples in the shale sand that are left after the tide goes out. It appears on many "hap shawls"—the less intricate shawls that the Shetland women made for their own use rather than for export. It's an easy stitch to commit to memory and use in a pinch again and again.

>> See pattern on page 31.

snaking trellis kneesocks

Lace has long been a favorite option for socks and leggings, which need to cling and expand to fit the leg. For these cozy woolen knee-highs, I've used a deceptively simple stitch pattern that combines Trellis with Stockinette. Worked in the round from the top down, the openwork stitches appear to move diagonally even while the same pattern round is repeated; the stitches then dramatically shift directions and form a complex-looking path of winding solid peaks. I've placed decreases within the stitch pattern that gently taper the solid and lace areas down to the ankle. In an undyed natural oat color, they are graphically patterned but subdued.

>> See pattern on page 32.

purse stitch cardigan with flower brooch

Purse stitch got its name because it was used for knitting the stocking (or miser's) purses that were a fad in England and France from the mid-eighteenth to the early twentieth centuries. Those tubular purses required a highly expandable stitch pattern such as this one. Purse stitch is also known as reverse faggoting, because it is worked with purled rather than knitted decreases. The rickrack mesh created with this easy, every-row repeat was noted as a favorite in *Mary Thomas's Book of Knitting Patterns* (which was first published in 1943).

Purse stitch has become a favorite of mine, too. For me, its strongly ridged yet delicately netted texture hits the right blend of rustic with feminine. Here, I use this quaint stitch for a cardigan with a vintage feel. On the lapel are flowers made with a picot knitting technique also found in Mary Thomas's book. The flowers are a fun accessory to knit up on their own and make quick party favors and gifts.

>> See pattern on page 35.

trellis beret and capelet

NOTE

To create the twisted cord for the Beret, cut one strand six times desired length. Fold strand(s) in half and secure one end to a stationary object. Twist folded strands from free end until they begin to buckle. Fold twisted length in half and holding ends together, allow to twist up on itself. Tie cut end in an overhand knot to secure.

STITCH PATTERN

Diagonal Trellis Pattern

(multiple of 2 sts; 1-rnd repeat)

All Rnds: *Yo, k2tog; repeat from * to end.

Note: When working this pattern, make sure not to forget to work each yarnover, or the pattern will not shift diagonally. When you work each k2tog, make sure that the yarnover from the previous rnd is to the right of the knit st on the left-hand needle; insert the right-hand needle through the knit st and under the arc of the yarnover, then knit them together. The k2togs will form diagonal columns that will slant to the right; since the pattern is the same on every rnd, the yarnovers will make single-strand ladders between the columns, much like dropped stitches.

SIZES

Beret: One size

Capelet: Small/Medium (Large, X-Large)

FINISHED MEASUREMENTS

Beret: 17 ¾" circumference, unstretched

Capelet: 35 ½ (39, 42 ¾)" shoulders; 53 ¼ (58 ¾, 64)" bottom edge

NOTE: Stitch pattern is very stretchy.

YARN

Crystal Palace Yarns Iceland (100% wool; 109 yards / 100 grams):

Beret: 1 ball #9719 Claret

Capelet: 3 (3, 4) balls #9719 Claret

NEEDLES

Beret: One 16" (40 cm) long circular (circ) needle size US 10 ½ (6.5 mm)

Capelet: One 16" (40 cm) long circular (circ) needle size US 10 ½ (6.5 mm)

One 29" (70 cm) long circular needle size US 10 ½ (6.5 mm)

Change needle size if necessary to obtain correct gauge.

NOTIONS

Stitch marker; ribbon for beret (optional)

GAUGE

9 sts and 9 rnds = 4" (10 cm) in Diagonal Trellis Pattern

Note: The gauge is 9 rnds if you measure along the diagonal slant of the pattern, or 14 rnds if you measure vertically. The measurements given in this pattern are vertical measurements.

BERET

Using 16" long circ needle and Long-Tail CO (see Special Techniques, page 154), CO 40 sts. Join for working in the rnd, being careful not to twist sts; pm for beginning of rnd. Begin Diagonal Trellis Pattern; work even for 4 rnds.

Increase Rnd: *Yo, [k1, yo] into yo from previous rnd but do not drop yo from left-hand needle, k2tog (second st on left-hand needle together with yo); repeat from * to end—80 sts.

Work even until piece measures 7".

Decrease Rnd 1: *Yo, k4tog [two (k1, yo) pairs]; repeat from * to end—40 sts remain. Work even for 8 rnds.

Decrease Rnd 2: *K2tog; repeat from * to end—20 sts. Knit 1 rnd.

Repeat Decrease Rnd 2 once—10 sts remain. Cut yarn, leaving long tail. Thread tail through remaining sts, pull tight and fasten off to WS.

FINISHING

Thread ribbon or twisted cord (optional) through yos 1½" up from CO edge. Block as desired.

CAPELET

Note: Piece is worked from the top down.

Using 16" long circ needle and Long-Tail CO (see Special Techniques, page 154), CO 40 (44, 48) sts. Join for working in the rnd, being careful not to twist sts; pm for beginning of rnd. Begin Diagonal Trellis Pattern; work even for 6 rnds.

Note: Change to longer circ needle when necessary for number of sts on needle.

Increase Rnd 1: *Yo, [k1, yo] into yo from previous rnd but do not drop yo from left-hand needle, k2tog (second st on left-hand needle together with yo); repeat from * to end—80 (88, 96) sts. Work even for 10 (13, 16) rnds.

Increase Rnd 2: *Yo, k2tog, yo, [k1, yo] into yo from previous rnd but do not drop yo from left-hand needle, k2tog (second st on left-hand needle together with yo); repeat from * to end—120 (132, 144) sts. Work even for 22 (25, 28) rnds. BO all sts knitwise.

FINISHING

Block as desired.

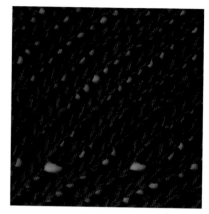

In Diagonal Trellis, the yarnover of the previous round is lifted and caught up in the decrease. Its front loop forms a rung of the ladder and its back loop is held behind, forming the left edge of each diagonal column. Note that the bias columns tilt 45 degrees to the right while the openwork strands appear to tilt 45 degrees to the left.

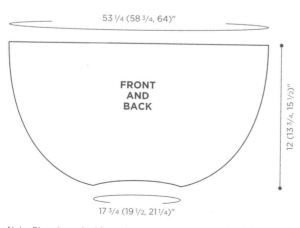

53 ¼ (58 ¾, 64)"

FRONT AND BACK

12 (13 ¾, 15 ½)"

17 ¾ (19 ½, 21 ¼)"

Note: Piece is worked from the top down. Because of weight of piece, length will grow slightly with wear.

butterfly lace tunic dress

SIZES
X-Small (Small, Medium, Large, X-Large, 2X-Large)

FINISHED MEASUREMENTS
30 3/4 (34, 37 1/4, 40 1/4, 43 1/2, 46 3/4)" bust

YARN
Loop-d-Loop by Teva Durham Quartz (54% viscose / 23% linen / 20% silk / 3% metallic; 103 yards / 50 grams): 10 (10, 11, 13, 14, 15) balls #04 Butter

NEEDLES
Two 24" (60 cm) long or longer circular (circ) needles size US 6 (4 mm)

Change needle size if necessary to obtain correct gauge.

NOTIONS
Stitch markers

GAUGE
20 sts and 24 rows = 4" (10 cm) in Stockinette st (St st)

18 sts and 22 1/2 rows = 4" (10 cm) in Butterfly Lace C from Chart

SKIRT
Using Long-Tail CO (see Special Techniques, page 154), CO 160 (176, 192, 208, 224, 240) sts. Join for working in the rnd, being careful not to twist sts; pm for beginning of rnd. *Note: Beginning of rnd is at back, before left side "seam."* Knit 1 rnd.

Next Rnd: Begin Butterfly Lace A from Chart. Work Rnds 1-8 three times, then Rnds 1-4 once.

Begin Side Lace Panel: *Work 12 sts of Butterfly Lace B from Chart, pm*, knit 68 (76, 84, 92, 100, 108), pm, repeat from * to * once, knit to end. Work even until piece measures 9" from the beginning.

Shape Waist: Decrease 4 sts this rnd, then every 6 rnds 4 times, as follows: [Work to marker, sm, k2tog, work to next marker, ssk, sm] twice—140 (156, 172, 188, 204, 220) sts. Work even until piece measures 16" from the beginning.

Shape Bust: Increase 4 sts this rnd, then every 6 rnds twice, as follows: [Work to marker, sm, k1-f/b, work to 2 sts before marker, k1-f/b, k1, sm] twice—152 (168, 184, 200, 216, 232) sts. Work even until piece measures 22" from the beginning, ending last rnd 2 sts past beginning of rnd marker.

BODICE
Divide for Front and Back: BO 8 sts, knit to next marker, removing marker, k2, place last 68 (76, 84, 92, 100, 108) sts on spare circ needle for Front, BO next 8 sts, knit to end—68 (76, 84, 92, 100, 108) sts remain each for Front and Back.

BACK
Working only on Back sts, purl 1 WS row.

Shape Armholes (RS): Continuing in St st, decrease 1 st each side this row, then every other row 7 times, as follows: Ssk, work to last 2 sts, k2tog—52 (60, 68, 76, 84, 92) sts remain. Work even until armhole measures 2 1/2 (3, 3 1/2, 4, 4 1/2, 5)", ending with a WS row. Change to Butterfly Lace C from Chart; work even until armhole measures 7 1/2 (8, 8 1/2, 9, 9 1/2, 10)", ending with a WS row. BO all sts knitwise.

FRONT

With WS facing, rejoin yarn to Front sts on spare circ needle. Work as for Back.

SLEEVES

Using Long-Tail CO, CO 56 (56, 56, 64, 64, 64) sts. Purl 1 row.

(RS) Begin Butterfly Lace C from Chart; work Rows 1–8 twice, then Rows 1–4 once.

Begin Center Lace Panel (RS): K22 (22, 22, 26, 26, 26), pm, work Butterfly Lace B across 12 sts, beginning with Row 5 of Chart, pm, knit to end. Work even for 5 rows.

Shape Sleeve (RS): Increase 1 st each side this row, then every 6 (6, 6, 4, 4, 4) rows 3 (5, 7, 6, 8, 10) times—64 (68, 72, 78, 82, 86) sts. Work even until piece measures 13" from the beginning, ending with a WS row.

Shape Cap (RS): BO 4 sts at beginning of next 2 rows, decrease 1 st each side every other row 13 (16, 17, 17, 18, 20) times, then every row 6 (4, 4, 6, 6, 6) times, as follows: On RS rows: K2, ssk, work to last 4 sts, k2tog, k2; on WS rows: P2, p2tog, work to last 4 sts, p2tog-tbl, p2. BO remaining 18 (20, 22, 24, 26, 26) sts.

FINISHING

Block pieces lightly with steam. Sew shoulder seams for ¾ (1¾, 2½, 3½, 4¼, 4¾)", leaving center 10 (10, 10, 10, 10, 11)" open for neck. Set in Sleeves, easing and gathering in top of Sleeve Cap. Sew Sleeve seams.

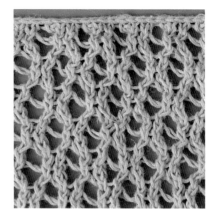

Alternately paired and opposing columns of decreases form hourglass outlines in Butterfly Lace. The open ovals are gracefully held ajar by loosely twisted double-yarnover strands.

BUTTERFLY LACE A

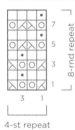

4-st repeat

BUTTERFLY LACE B

BUTTERFLY LACE C

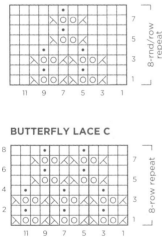

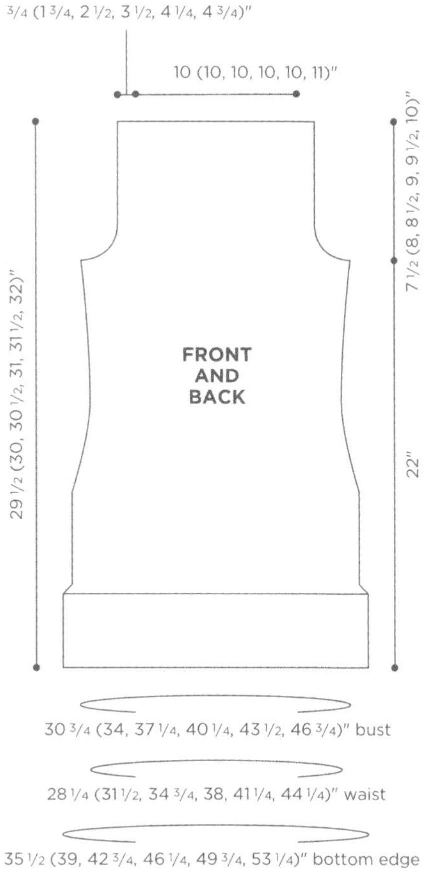

4-st repeat

KEY

- ☐ Knit on RS, purl on WS.
- • Purl on RS, knit on WS.
- ☐ Yo
- ◲ K2tog
- ◳ Ssk

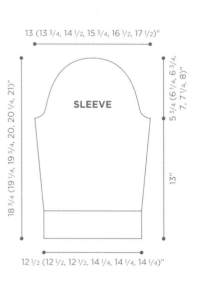

¾ (1¾, 2½, 3½, 4¼, 4¾)"

10 (10, 10, 10, 10, 11)"

7½ (8, 8½, 9, 9½, 10)"

29½ (30, 30½, 31, 31½, 32)"

FRONT AND BACK

22"

30¾ (34, 37¼, 40¼, 43½, 46¾)" bust

28¼ (31½, 34¾, 38, 41¼, 44¼)" waist

35½ (39, 42¾, 46¼, 49¾, 53¼)" bottom edge

13 (13¾, 14½, 15¾, 16½, 17½)"

5¾ (6¼, 6¾, 7, 7½, 8)"

SLEEVE

18¾ (19¼, 19¾, 20, 20¼, 21)"

13"

12½ (12½, 12½, 14¼, 14¼, 14¼)"

portcullis jacket

NOTES

Knotted CO: *Note: This CO is based on the Long-Tail CO.* Leaving tail with about 1" of yarn for each st to be cast-on, make a slipknot in the yarn and place it on the right-hand needle, with the tail to the front and the working end to the back. Insert the thumb and forefinger of your left hand between the strands of yarn so that the working end is around your forefinger, and the tail end is around your thumb "slingshot" fashion; *insert the tip of the right-hand needle into the front loop on the thumb, hook the strand of yarn coming from the forefinger from back to front, and draw it through the loop on your thumb; remove your thumb from the loop and pull on the working yarn to tighten the new stitch on the right-hand needle*; pass the slipknot over the last stitch and off the needle to bind off one stitch. Repeat from * to * twice; pass the next-to-last stitch over the last stitch and off the needle to bind off one stitch. Continue in this manner, casting on two stitches and binding off one, until you have the number of stitches required.

STITCH PATTERN

Portcullis Stitch

(multiple of 4 sts + 1; 2-row repeat)

Row 1 (RS): K2tog, *[k1, yo, k1] in next st, sk2p; repeat from * to last 3 sts, [k1, yo, k1] in next st, ssk.

Row 2: Purl.

Repeat Rows 1 and 2 for Portcullis Stitch.

SIZES

To fit bust sizes 31-33 (35-37, 39-41, 43-45, 45-47, 49-51)"

X-Small (Small, Medium, Large, X-Large, 2X-Large)

FINISHED MEASUREMENTS

29 1/4 (32 3/4, 36 1/2, 40, 43 3/4, 47 1/4)" bust, including zipper

Note: Stitch pattern can stretch significantly.

YARN

Loop-d-Loop by Teva Durham Moss (85% extrafine merino wool / 15% nylon; 163 yards / 50 grams): 6 (7, 8, 8, 9, 10) balls #06 Indigo

NEEDLES

One 29" (70 cm) long circular (circ) needle size US 6 (4 mm)

One 29" (70 cm) long circular needle size US 7 (4.5 mm)

One 29" (70 cm) long circular needle size US 8 (5 mm)

Change needle size if necessary to obtain correct gauge.

NOTIONS

Stitch markers; stitch holders; two 7/8" buttons (plus additional buttons if desired, for straps); 2 snaps for pocket flaps; metal separating zipper 24 (24 1/2, 25, 25 1/2, 26, 26 1/2)" long, to match buttons *(Note: Zipper may be cut down to fit Fronts.)*

GAUGE

24 sts and 21 rows = 4" (10 cm) in Portcullis Stitch, using size US 6 needle

22 sts and 22 rows = 4" (10 cm) in Portcullis Stitch, using size US 7 needle

20 sts and 22 rows = 4" (10 cm) in Portcullis Stitch, using size US 8 needle

BODY

Using size US 7 circ needle and Knotted CO, CO 156 (176, 196, 216, 236, 256) sts. Change to size US 8 circ needle. Purl 1 row, decrease 1 st at middle of row—155 (175, 195, 215, 235, 255) sts remain.

Row 1 (RS): *Note: Faux "seams" will be worked up the Fronts, where the pockets will be.* K2tog, [(k1, yo, k1) in next st, sk2p] 3 (3, 4, 4, 5, 5) times, (k1, yo, k1) in next st, k2tog, pm for "seam," ssk, [(k1, yo, k1) in next st, sk2p] 29 (34, 37, 42, 45, 50) times, [k1, yo, k1] in next st, k2tog, pm for "seam," ssk, [(k1, yo, k1) in next st, sk2p] 3 (3, 4, 4, 5, 5) times, [k1, yo, k1] in next st, ssk.

Row 2: Purl.

Work even until piece measures 4″ from the beginning, ending with a WS row.

Shape Body (RS): Change to size US 7 circ needle; work even until piece measures 8″ from the beginning, ending with a WS row.

Shape Pocket Openings (RS) (optional): *Note: If you prefer not to work pocket opening, skip to **.* Work to first marker, join a second ball of yarn, work to second marker, join a third ball of yarn, work to end. Working all three sections at the same time, **work even until piece measures 10″ from the beginning, ending with a WS row.

Shape Waist (RS): Change to size US 6 circ needle; work even until piece measures 4″ from beginning of pocket openings, or 12″ from cast-on edge if pockets were omitted, ending with a WS row. Break second and third balls of yarn.

Close Pocket Openings (RS): Change to size US 7 circ needle; work across all sts with first ball of yarn. Work even until piece measures 16 (16, 16 1/2, 16 1/2, 17, 17)″ from the beginning, ending with a RS row.

Divide Fronts and Back (WS): P38 (38, 46, 46, 46, 46) sts, BO next 7 (15, 15, 23, 31, 39) sts, p64 (68, 72, 76, 80, 84) (not including st remaining on

In Portcullis, ridged columns of double decreases create textural vertical stripes in which the stitches appear braided or folded upon themselves. The textured columns alternate with furroughs of twined, open mesh.

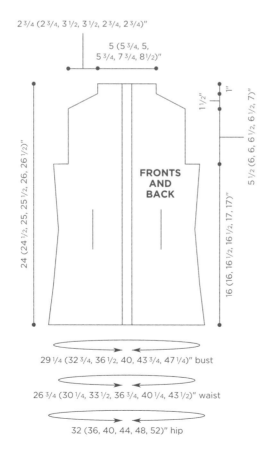

2 3/4 (2 3/4, 3 1/2, 3 1/2, 2 3/4, 2 3/4)″

5 (5 3/4, 5, 5 3/4, 7 3/4, 8 1/2)″

1 1/2″

1″

5 1/2 (6, 6, 6 1/2, 6 1/2, 7)″

FRONTS AND BACK

24 (24 1/2, 25, 25 1/2, 26, 26 1/2)″

16 (16, 16 1/2, 16 1/2, 17, 17)″

29 1/4 (32 3/4, 36 1/2, 40, 43 3/4, 47 1/4)″ bust

26 3/4 (30 1/4, 33 1/2, 36 3/4, 40 1/4, 43 1/2)″ waist

32 (36, 40, 44, 48, 52)″ hip

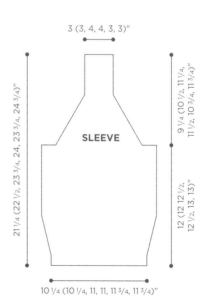

3 (3, 4, 4, 3, 3)″

SLEEVE

9 1/4 (10 1/2, 11 1/4, 11 1/2, 10 3/4, 11 3/4)″

21 1/4 (22 1/2, 23 3/4, 24, 23 3/4, 24 3/4)″

12 (12 12 1/2, 12 1/2, 13, 13)″

10 1/4 (10 1/4, 11, 11, 11 3/4, 11 3/4)″

right-hand needle after last BO), BO next 7 (15, 15, 23, 31, 39) sts, purl to end—38 (38, 46, 46, 46, 46) sts remain each Front; 65 (69, 73, 77, 81, 85) sts remain for Back. Place sts for Back and Left Front on holder.

RIGHT FRONT

(RS) Work in pattern as established to last 2 sts, ssk. Work even until armhole measures 5 1/2 (6, 6, 6 1/2, 6 1/2, 7)", ending with a WS row.

Shape Shoulders: *Note: Shoulders are shaped using short rows (see Special Techniques, page 154).*

Rows 1 (RS) and 2: Work to last 7 sts, wrp-t, work to end.

Rows 3-8: Work to 3 sts before wrapped st of row before last row worked, wrp-t, work to end—34 (34, 42, 42, 42, 42) sts remain after Row 7.

Row 9: Work in pattern as established, working wraps together with wrapped sts as you come to them.

Row 10: BO 15 (15, 19, 19, 15, 15) sts purlwise—19 (19, 23, 23, 27, 27) sts remain.

Row 11: Work to last 2 sts, k2. Work even until piece measures 1" from shoulder BO, ending with a WS row. BO all sts knitwise.

LEFT FRONT

With RS facing, rejoin yarn to sts on hold for Left Front. K2tog, work to end. Work even until armhole measures 5 1/2 (6, 6, 6 1/2, 6 1/2, 7)", ending with a RS row.

Shape Shoulders: *Note: Shoulders are shaped using short rows.*

Rows 1 (WS) and 2: Work to last 7 sts, wrp-t, work to end.

Rows 3-8: Work to 3 sts before wrapped st of row before last row worked, wrp-t, work to end—34 (34, 42, 42, 42, 42) sts remain after Row 7.

Row 9: Work in pattern as established to marker, purl to end, working wraps together with wrapped sts as you come to them.

Row 10: BO 15 (15, 19, 19, 15, 15) sts knitwise—19 (19, 23, 23, 27, 27) sts remain. Purl 1 row.

Row 11: K2, work to end. Work even until piece measures 1" from shoulder BO, ending with a WS row. BO all sts knitwise.

BACK

With RS facing, rejoin yarn to sts on hold for Back. K2tog, work to last 2 sts, ssk. Work even until armholes measure 5 1/2 (6, 6, 6 1/2, 6 1/2, 7)", ending with a WS row.

Shape Shoulders: *Note: Shoulders are shaped using short rows.*

Rows 1 (RS) and 2: Work to last 7 sts, wrp-t.

Rows 3-8: Work to 3 sts before wrapped st of row before last row worked, wrp-t—57 (61, 65, 69, 73, 77) sts remain after Row 7.

Rows 9 and 10: Knit to marker, working wraps together with wrapped sts as you come to them, work in pattern as established to next marker, knit to end, working wraps together with wrapped sts as you come to them.

Row 11: BO 15 (15, 19, 19, 15, 15) sts knitwise, k1, work to marker, knit to end.

Row 12: BO 15 (15, 19, 19, 15, 15) sts purlwise, purl to end—27 (31, 27, 31, 43, 47) sts remain. Work even until piece measures 1" from shoulder BO, ending with a WS row. BO all sts knitwise.

SLEEVES

Using size US 7 circ needle and Knotted CO, CO 58 (58, 62, 62, 66, 66) sts. Purl 1 row, decrease 1 st at middle of row—57 (57, 61, 61, 65, 65) sts remain. Begin Portcullis Stitch; work even for 6 rows.

Shape Sleeve (RS): Increase 1 st each side this row, then every 6 rows 3 times, as follows: K2tog, M1, work to last 2 sts, M1, ssk—65 (65, 69, 69, 73, 73) sts. *Note: Work increased sts in St st until you have completed all 4 increases, then work increased sts in Portcullis Stitch.*

Work even until piece measures 12 (12, 12 1/2, 12 1/2, 13, 13)" from the beginning, ending with a WS row.

Shape Cap (RS): BO 4 (8, 8, 12, 16, 20) sts at beginning of next 2 rows—57 (49, 53, 45, 41, 33) sts remain.

(RS) K2tog, work to last 2 sts, ssk. Purl 1 row.

Decrease Row (RS): Continuing in Portcullis Stitch, decrease 4 sts each side this row, then every 6 (10, 10, 16, 16, 36) rows 4 (3, 3, 2, 2, 1) time(s), as follows: K3tog-tbl, sk2p, work to last 6 sts, sk2p, k3tog—17 (17, 21, 21, 17, 17) sts remain. *Note: On RS rows following Decrease Rows, work first 2 sts of row as k2tog, and last 2 sts as ssk.*

Work even until piece measures 9 1/4 (10 1/2, 11 1/4, 11 1/2, 10 3/4, 11 3/4)" from beginning of cap shaping, ending with a WS row. BO all sts knitwise.

FINISHING

Block as desired. Set in Sleeves, sewing straight section of top of Sleeve cap to shoulder and neck. Sew Sleeve seams. Sew zipper to Fronts.

POCKET FLAPS (make 2)

Using size US 7 circ needle, CO 23 sts. Begin Garter st (knit every row); work even for 1 1/2".

Shape Flap (RS): Decrease 1 st each side this row, then every other row 5 times, as follows: Ssk, knit to last 2 sts, k2tog—11 sts remain. BO all sts. Sew CO edge of Pocket Flap to edge of pocket opening nearest center Front, or to knit column nearest center Front, 8" up from bottom edge, if you chose not to work pocket openings. Sew button to narrow edge of Pocket Flap, 1" in from BO edge. Sew half of one snap to WS of Pocket Flap and other half of snap to Front.

SHOULDER/BACK STRAPS (make 3)

Using size US 7 circ needle, CO 7 sts. Begin Garter st; work even until piece measures 4". BO all sts. Sew 1 Strap to top of each Sleeve cap, and 1 centered on Back, 10 (10, 10 1/2, 10 1/2, 11, 11)" up from bottom edge. Sew additional buttons to Straps if desired.

old shale belt

NOTE

Twisted stitches are used within the stitch pattern so the leather cord does not slip out of place. Stretch the piece lengthwise from time to time so that the cord will not bend on itself, and you can measure the true length.

STITCH PATTERN

Old Shale Variation
(panel of 11 sts; 4-row repeat)

Row 1 (RS): [K2tog] twice, [yo, k1-tbl] 3 times, yo, [ssk] twice.

Row 2: P3, [p1-tbl, p1] 3 times, p2.

Row 3: K3, [k1-tbl, k1] 3 times, k2.

Row 4: Knit.

Repeat Rows 1-4 for Old Shale Variation.

BELT

CO 11 sts, leaving 12" long tail for sewing buckle. Knit 1 row.

(RS) Begin Old Shale Variation; work even until piece measures 33", or to 4" longer than desired length for waist or hip, ending with Row 4 of pattern. BO all sts purlwise.

FINISHING

With tail, sew buckle shank to CO edge.

FINISHED MEASUREMENTS

2 1/2" wide x 33" long

Note: Belt can be made to fit any desired measurement. Simply measure waist or hip and add 4" for final Belt length.

MATERIALS

Leather Cord (1 mm round / 100 yards): 1 spool white with pearl finish

Note: This cord is commonly available at beading and trimming stores.

NEEDLES

One pair straight needles size US 5 (3.75 mm)

Change needle size if necessary to obtain correct gauge.

NOTIONS

2 1/4" round buckle with center shank

GAUGE

11 sts and 15 rows = 2 1/2" (6 cm) in Old Shale Variation

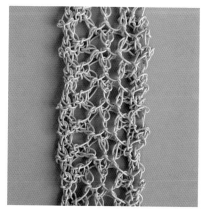

The arches of Old Shale stack up as they are worked, creating four windows between five posts.

snaking trellis kneesocks

SIZES
Small/Medium (Medium/
Large)

FINISHED
MEASUREMENTS
7 3/4" Foot circumference

11 (12)" Leg circumference,
unstretched

9 (10)" Foot length from
back of Heel

18" Leg length to base of
Heel

YARN
Lion Brand Yarns LB 1878
(100% wool; 2045 yards /
500 grams): 1 cone #098
Natural Heather

*Note: One cone will make
3 pair.*

NEEDLES
One set of five double-
pointed needles (dpn)
size US 2 (2.75 mm)

Change needle size if necessary to obtain correct gauge.

NOTIONS
Stitch markers; waste yarn

GAUGE
25 sts and 43 rnds = 4"
(10 cm) in Zigzag Trellis –
Right Sock from Chart

24 sts and 36 rnds = 4"
(10 cm) in Stockinette stitch
(St st)

NOTES

These Socks are worked from the top down, with Leg shaping worked within the pattern repeats. The Zig-zag Trellis pattern for Left and Right Socks is mirrored. Rather than a more complex short-row turned heel, a row of stitches is knit in waste yarn as a placeholder for the Heel, which will be worked once the Foot is complete.

The pattern is written so that both sizes have the same number of stitches for the Foot, since the Trellis pattern will allow the Foot to fit a range of sizes. Instructions are included for working a slightly larger Foot circumference for the size Medium/Large, if desired.

STITCH PATTERN

1x1 Rib

(multiple of 2 sts)

All Rnds: *K1, p1; repeat from * to end.

RIGHT SOCK

Leg

Using working yarn, CO 72 (78) sts. Divide sts evenly among 4 needles [18-18-18-18 (19-20-19-20)]. Join for working in the rnd, being careful not to twist sts; pm for beginning of rnd. Begin 1x1 Rib; work even for 1". Change to Zigzag Trellis—Right Sock from Chart; work even through Rnd 169 of Chart, working decreases as indicated—48 sts remain. *Note: If you are working size Medium/Large and prefer a slightly larger foot circumfer-ence, omit the decreases on Rnd 169 of Chart (54 sts remain) and work the 9-st repeat for the Zigzag Trellis—Instep Chart.*

Next Rnd: Knit, repositioning sts if necessary so that you have 12 sts on each needle, 24 sts each for sole and instep. *Note: If you are working on 54 sts, reposition the sts if necessary so that you have 12 sts each on the sole needles and 15 sts each on the instep needles, with Trellis Pattern centered on instep needles.*

Insert Heel Placeholder: Needles 1 and 2: Cut working yarn, join waste yarn, knit to end, cut waste yarn; **Needles 3 and 4:** Rejoin working yarn, work Zigzag Trellis—Instep from Chart to end.

Foot

Next Rnd: Needles 1 and 2: Knit; **Needles 3 and 4:** Work Zigzag Trellis—Instep. Continuing in St st over sole sts and Zigzag Trellis—Instep over instep sts, work even until piece measures 6 1/2 (7 1/2)" from Heel placeholder, or 2 1/2" less than desired length from back of Heel. *Note: Half of the 2 1/2" is for Toe shaping, and half is for Heel shaping, to be worked after the Toe is completed.* Knit 1 rnd. *Note: If you are working on 54 sts, decrease 6 sts evenly across the instep sts, so that you now have 24 sts each for sole and instep.*

Toe

Decrease Rnd: Needle 1: Ssk, knit to end; **Needle 2:** Knit to last 2 sts, k2tog; **Needles 3 and 4:** Repeat Needles 1 and 2—44 sts remain. Knit 1 rnd. Repeat Decrease Rnd every other rnd 4 times—28 sts remain. Cut yarn, leaving long tail. Transfer sts from Needle 2 onto Needle 1 and sts from Needle 4 onto Needle 3. Using Kitchener st (see Special Techniques, page 155), graft Toe sts.

Heel

Carefully remove waste yarn and place bottom 24 sts (closest to Leg) and top 23 sts (closest to Foot) onto 4 dpns (12-12-12-11)—47 sts. Join for working in the rnd; pm for beginning of rnd. Knit to end, pick up and knit 1 st—48 sts (12-12-12-12). Complete as for Toe.

LEFT SOCK
Leg

Work as for Right Sock through Rnd 169 of Chart, working Zigzag Trellis—Left Sock from Chart—48 sts remain.

Next Rnd: Knit to last st, reposition marker to before last st for new beginning of rnd. You now have 24 sts each for instep and sole. Reposition sts if necessary so that you have 12 sts on each needle. *Note: If you are working on 54 sts, reposition the sts if necessary so that you have 12 sts each on the sole needles and 15 sts each on the instep needles, with Trellis Pattern centered on instep needles.*

Insert Heel Placeholder: Needles 1 and 2: Work Zigzag Trellis—Instep from Chart to end, cut working yarn; **Needles 3 and 4:** Join waste yarn, knit to end, cut waste yarn.

Foot

Next Rnd: Needles 1 and 2: Rejoin working yarn, work Zigzag Trellis—Instep; **Needles 3 and 4:** Knit. Continuing in Zigzag Trellis—Instep over instep sts and St st over sole sts, complete as for Right Sock.

FINISHING
Block as desired.

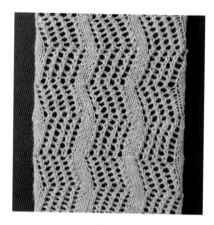

Zigzag Trellis columns feature open rungs of tight twists; each twist is formed when the yarnover of the lace round is worked plain on the next round and then that stitch is caught into the decrease of the following lace round. The trellis changes orientation every 12 rounds, creating biases in the other direction and forcing the columns of Stockinette stitch to curve.

ZIGZAG TRELLIS - RIGHT SOCK

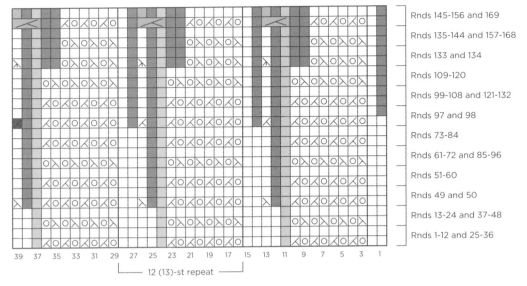

Rnds 145-156 and 169
Rnds 135-144 and 157-168
Rnds 133 and 134
Rnds 109-120
Rnds 99-108 and 121-132
Rnds 97 and 98
Rnds 73-84
Rnds 61-72 and 85-96
Rnds 51-60
Rnds 49 and 50
Rnds 13-24 and 37-48
Rnds 1-12 and 25-36

39 37 35 33 31 29 27 25 23 21 19 17 15 13 11 9 7 5 3 1

└── 12 (13)-st repeat ──┘

ZIGZAG TRELLIS - LEFT SOCK

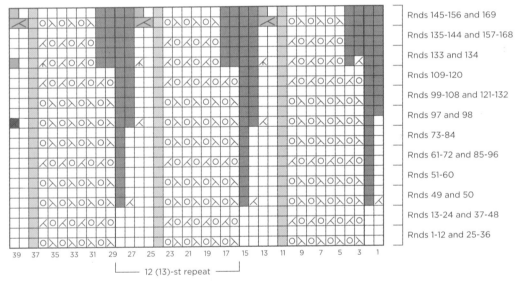

Rnds 145-156 and 169
Rnds 135-144 and 157-168
Rnds 133 and 134
Rnds 109-120
Rnds 99-108 and 121-132
Rnds 97 and 98
Rnds 73-84
Rnds 61-72 and 85-96
Rnds 51-60
Rnds 49 and 50
Rnds 13-24 and 37-48
Rnds 1-12 and 25-36

39 37 35 33 31 29 27 25 23 21 19 17 15 13 11 9 7 5 3 1

└── 12 (13)-st repeat ──┘

ZIGZAG TRELLIS - INSTEP

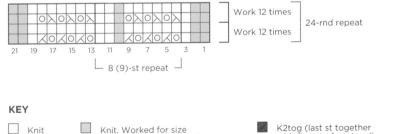

Work 12 times
Work 12 times
} 24-rnd repeat

21 19 17 15 13 11 9 7 5 3 1

└── 8 (9)-st repeat ──┘

KEY

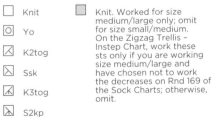

☐ Knit

◯ Yo

☑ K2tog

☒ Ssk

☒ K3tog

☒ S2kp

Knit. Worked for size medium/large only; omit for size small/medium. On the Zigzag Trellis – Instep Chart, work these sts only if you are working size medium/large and have chosen not to work the decreases on Rnd 169 of the Sock Charts; otherwise, omit.

K2tog (last st together with first st of next rnd); reposition beginning of rnd marker to after k2tog.

Knit first st of next rnd; reposition beginning of rnd marker to after this st.

No stitch if you worked the blue decreases in the previous rnd; otherwise, work as knit.

☑ or ☒ K2tog. Worked on Rnd 169 for size medium/large only; size small/medium and all other rnds, work as knit. If you prefer a slightly larger foot circumference, omit this decrease and work as k2. You will then have to work a 9-st repeat on the Zigzag Trellis – Instep Chart.

purse stitch cardigan with flower brooch

NOTES

Waistband and Cuffs are worked side-to-side; the Waistband has curved cutaway shaping worked with increases and decreases at the front, and the Cuffs have a slight bell shape worked with short rows. The Body is worked in one piece from the Waistband to the armholes, then the Sleeves are joined and the raglan Yoke is worked in one piece to the neck.

Knitted CO: Make a loop (using a slip knot) with the working yarn and place it on the left-hand needle (first st CO), *knit into the st on the left-hand needle, draw up a loop but do not drop st from left-hand needle; place new loop on left-hand needle; repeat from * for remaining sts to be CO, or for casting on at the end of a row in progress.

STITCH PATTERNS

Garter Ridge Pattern
(any number of sts; 6-row repeat)

Row 1 (WS): Knit.

Rows 2-4: Knit.

Row 5: Purl.

Row 6: Knit.

Repeat Rows 1-6 for Garter Ridge Pattern.

Purse Stitch
(even number of sts; 1-row repeat)

All Rows: K1, *yo, p2tog; repeat from * to last st, k1.

Note: When working this pattern, make sure not to forget to work each yarnover. When you work each p2tog, purl together the knit st with the yarnover to its left.

SIZES
X-Small (Small, Medium, Large, X-Large, 2X-Large)

FINISHED MEASUREMENTS
34 1/4 (37, 40, 43, 45 3/4, 48 3/4)" bust, slightly stretched

YARN
Loop-d-Loop by Teva Durham Birch (65% cotton / 35% silk; 98 yards / 50 grams): 7 (9, 10, 11, 12, 13) balls #03 Dove Grey (MC); 1 (2, 2, 2, 2, 3) ball(s) #11 Aqua (A)
Small amount white worsted weight yarn for flower centers (B)

NEEDLES
One pair straight needles size US 6 (4 mm)
One 29" (70 cm) long circular (circ) needle size 7 (4.5 mm)
Change needle size if necessary to obtain correct gauge.

NOTIONS
Stitch markers; stitch holders or spare needles

GAUGE
20 sts and 30 rows = 4" (10 cm) in Garter Ridge Pattern, using smaller needles, slightly stretched
11 sts and 20 rows = 4" (10 cm) in Purse Stitch, using larger needle, slightly stretched

WAISTBAND

Using smaller needles and A, CO 15 sts. Begin Garter Ridge Pattern; work even for 1", ending with a WS row.

Shape Waistband (RS): Continuing in Garter Ridge Pattern, increase 1 st at end of this row, then every 6 rows 4 times—20 sts. Work even until piece measures 21 (23 3/4, 26 1/4, 29, 31 3/4, 34 1/4)" from the beginning, ending with a WS row.

(RS) Decrease 1 st at end of this row, then every 6 rows 4 times—15 sts. Work even until piece measures 26 (28 3/4, 31 1/4, 34, 36 3/4, 39 1/4)" from the beginning, slightly stretched, ending with a WS row. BO all sts.

BODY

With RS of Waistband facing, using larger needle and B, pick up and knit 78 (86, 94, 102, 110, 118) sts along straight side edge of Waistband. Begin Purse stitch; work even until piece measures 6" from base of Waistband, measured at the center Back, ending with a WS row. Place markers 19 (21, 23, 25, 27, 29) sts in from each edge, making sure to count each yo as a st.

Shape Bust (RS): Increase 4 sts this row, then every 6 rows 3 times, as follows: Work in Purse stitch to 2 sts before marker, [yo, p1] twice, sm, work to next marker, sm, [yo, p1] twice, work to end—94 (102, 110, 118, 126, 134) sts; 23 (25, 27, 29, 31, 33) sts each Front, 48 (52, 56, 60, 64, 68) sts for Back. Work even until piece measures 13" from base of Waistband, measured at the center Back, ending with a WS (WS, WS, RS, RS, RS) row.

SIZES LARGE, X-LARGE, 2X-LARGE ONLY

Shape Armhole (WS): Work to (—, —, 6, 8, 8) sts before marker, BO next (—, —, 4, 8, 8) sts, work to (—, —, 6, 8, 8) sts before next marker, BO next (—, —, 4, 8, 8) sts, work to end— (—, —, 27, 27, 29) sts remain each Front, (—, —, 56, 56, 60) sts for Back.

ALL SIZES: Transfer sts to st holders or spare needle. Set aside; do not cut yarn.

LEFT CUFF

Using smaller needles and A, CO 15 sts. Begin Garter Ridge Pattern; work even until piece measures 8 (8, 8, 9, 9, 9)" from the beginning, ending with a WS row.

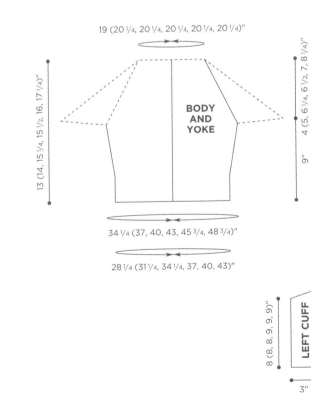

WAISTBAND

4"

3"

17 1/2 (20 1/4, 22 3/4, 25 1/2, 28 1/4, 30 3/4,)"

26 (28 3/4, 31 1/4, 34, 36 3/4, 39 1/4)"

19 (20 1/4, 20 1/4, 20 1/4, 20 1/4, 20 1/4)"

BODY AND YOKE

13 (14, 15 1/4, 15 1/2, 16, 17 1/4)"

9"

4 (5, 6 1/4, 6 1/2, 7, 8 1/4)"

34 1/4 (37, 40, 43, 45 3/4, 48 3/4)"

28 1/4 (31 1/4, 34 1/4, 37, 40, 43)"

LEFT CUFF

3"

8 (8, 8, 9, 9)"

9 1/2 (9 1/2, 9 1/2, 10 1/2, 10 1/2, 10 1/2)"

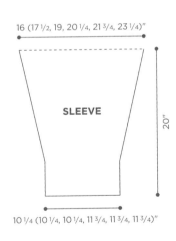

SLEEVE

16 (17 1/2, 19, 20 1/4, 21 3/4, 23 1/4)"

20"

10 1/4 (10 1/4, 10 1/4, 11 3/4, 11 3/4, 11 3/4)"

Shape Cuff: *Note: Cuff is shaped using short rows (see Special Techniques, page 154).*

Rows 1 (RS) and 2 (WS): Work 12 sts, wrp-t, work to end.

Rows 3-8: Work to 3 sts before wrapped st of row before last row worked, wrp-t, work to end.

Row 9: Work even, working wraps together with wrapped sts as you come to them. BO all sts.

RIGHT CUFF

Work as for Left Cuff, reversing all shaping, and beginning short row shaping with a WS row.

SLEEVES

With RS of Cuff facing, using larger needle and B, pick up and knit 28 (28, 28, 32, 32, 32) sts along shorter of two long edges of Cuff.

(WS) *Yo, p2tog; repeat from * to end. Work even until piece measures 4" from pick-up row, ending with a WS row.

Shape Sleeve (RS): Increase 2 sts each side this row, every 8 rows 3 (4, 5, 5, 4, 4) times, then every 6 rows 0 (0, 0, 0, 2, 3) times, as follows: [Yo, p1] twice, work to last 2 sts, [yo, p1] twice—44 (48, 52, 56, 60, 64) sts. *Note: Work increased sts in pattern as they become available.* Work even until piece measures 20" from base of Cuff, ending with a WS row.

Shape Cap (RS): BO 0 (0, 0, 2, 4, 4) sts at beginning of next 2 rows. Place remaining 44 (48, 52, 52, 52, 56) sts on holder or spare needle for Yoke.

YOKE

Join Pieces (RS): Work across 23 (25, 27, 27, 27, 29) sts for Right Front, pm, 44 (48, 52, 52, 52, 56) sts from holder for Right Sleeve, pm, 48 (52, 56, 56, 56, 60) sts for Back, pm, 44 (48, 52, 52, 52, 56) sts for Left Sleeve, pm, then 23 (25, 27, 27, 27, 29) sts for Left Front—182 (198, 214, 214, 214, 230) sts. Work even for 1 row.

Shape Yoke

Decrease Row 1 (RS): [Work to 2 sts before marker, p2tog, remove marker, p2tog, pm] 4 times, work to end—174 (190, 206, 206, 206, 222) sts remain. Work even for 1 row.

Decrease Row 2 (RS): [Work to 2 sts before marker, pm, p2tog, remove marker, p2tog] 4 times, work to end—166 (182, 198, 198, 198, 214) sts remain. Work even for 1 row.

Repeat Decrease Rows 1 and 2 two (3, 4, 4, 4, 5) times, then repeat Decrease Row 1 one (0, 0, 0, 0, 0) time(s)—110 (118, 118, 118, 118, 118) sts remain. Work even for 0 (2, 4, 6, 8, 10) rows.

Shape Neck

Decrease Row 1 (RS): K1, [yo, p2tog] 8 (7, 7, 7, 7, 7) times, [p2tog] 14 (16, 16, 16, 16, 16) times, [yo, p2tog] 14 (12, 12, 12, 12, 12) times, [p2tog] 14 (16, 16, 16, 16, 16) times, [yo, p2tog] 8 (7, 7, 7, 7, 7) times, k1—82 (86, 86, 86, 86, 86) sts remain.

Decrease Row 2 (WS): K1, [yo, p2tog] 5 (6, 6, 6, 6, 6) times, [p2tog] 10 times, [yo, p2tog] 10 times, [p2tog] 10 times, [yo, p2tog] 5 (6, 6, 6, 6, 6) times, k1—62 (66, 66, 66, 66, 66) sts remain.

Decrease Row 3 (RS): K1, [yo, p2tog] 5 (6, 6, 6, 6, 6) times, [with left needle, lift strand from row below, p3tog (lifted strand with next 2 sts)] 5 times, [yo, p2tog] 10 times, [p3tog (lifted strand from row below with next 2 sts)] 5 times, [yo, p2tog] 5 (6, 6, 6, 6, 6) times, k1—52 (56, 56, 56, 56, 56) sts remain. BO all sts.

FINISHING

Sew Sleeve seams.

FLOWER BROOCH (make 2)

Center: Using smaller needles and B, make a slipknot and place on left-hand needle, *using Knitted CO (see Special Techniques, page 154), CO 3 sts. BO 3 sts—1 st remains. Repeat from* 4 times to form 5 picots on a chain. Join into a ring by picking up and knitting 1 st into base of first picot. BO 1 st. Cut yarn and fasten off.

In Purse stitch, the same pattern row is worked in the opposite direction on alternate rows, creating a rickrack wavering of stitch columns and nubby Garter stitch texture.

Petals: Using MC, pick up and knit 1 st between 2 picots.

*Row 1 (WS): K1-f/b—2 sts.

Rows 2, 4, 6, 8, and 10: Knit.

Rows 3, 5, and 7: Knit to last st, k1-f/b—5 sts after Row 7.

Rows 9 and 11: Knit.

Rows 12, 14, and 16: BO 1 st, knit to end—2 sts remain after Row 16.

Rows 13, 15, and 17: Knit.

Row 18: BO 1 st—1 st remains. Do not turn. Pick up and knit 1 st between next 2 picots to the left of where current Petal is attached—2 sts. BO 1 st—1 st remains.

Repeat from * 4 times. Fasten off remaining st.

Repeat for second Flower, working Petals in A. Sew center of each Flower to Right Front (see photo).

Block as desired.

EYELETS

Decorative and Functional Holes

THIS CHAPTER PRESENTS A VARIETY OF PROJECTS THAT FEATURE SOLID fabrics dotted with holes—or eyelets—placed in strategic designs. In knitting, an eyelet is formed when a yarnover is treated as a stitch on the following row rather than dropped. Technically speaking, the eyelet hole is the gap at the center of the yarnover loop. Because the yarnover creates a new stitch, a decrease is typically worked in conjunction to keep a consistent stitch number and fabric width. The decrease serves to frame the eyelet and seems to shore up the structure of its edge while holding it open. One can easily imagine that the eyelet was discovered by accident. As new knitters we often mistakenly create holes by wrapping the yarn over the needle as if to knit but neglect to pull it through the stitch, only to discover a hole and an extra stitch several rows later. Perhaps this happened to one of our knitting forebears, and perhaps this knitter then recalled and refined the trick to make holes with a decorative intention.

The word "eyelet" is a translation of the fourteenth-century French word *oillet*, meaning "little eye." Many knitted eyelet patterns are reminiscent of "white work" textiles used in home linens and nightgowns, as well as embroidered eyelet cloth, called *broderie Anglaise*, which features cut holes that have been embellished around the edges. Knitting stitch dictionaries contain a variety of eyelet patterns seemingly drawn from this textile tradition. The stitch pattern I've used for the Rose Trellis Blouse (see opposite and page 55) is one example.

While eyelets can be used to create fascinating surface designs with positive and negative space, they are more than just decoration. Eyelets have a history of being functional, allowing for ribbons and drawstrings to be run through them to provide adjustable closures (as you'll find in the Lace Puff Bloomers on page 58). They can also be used as a shaping mechanism without the standard matched number of decreases, as I've explored in the Top-Down Eyelet T-Shirt on page 48. Sometimes eyelets can be used to achieve a three-dimensional effect; if the decrease is pointed outward, away from the eyelet, it forms a stronger "outline," which can contribute significantly to this illusion. When decreases are stacked strategically to form longer lines, they can draw shapes, such as the chevrons on the Chevron Eyelet Skirt on page 50, and complex graphics as seen on the Interlocking Squares Pillow and Bolster on page 52.

top-down eyelet t-shirt

This project was inspired by the ballet T-shirts in my first book, *Loop-d-Loop*. Those mother/daughter, top-down, knit-in-the-round shirts have been an easy favorite among knitters—even a class of seven-year-olds are knitting the ballet tee at Tante Sophie's knitting studio in Boonton, New Jersey. Here is an equally quick and quirky project that can be adjusted to fit gals of all ages. Rather than working raglan increases, eyelets around the neckline serve as increases, radiating down the yoke while adding a decorative textural accent. And instead of a standard open eyelet, this is more like a tuck stitch—the yarnovers are slipped for several rows and then all the floats are knit together at once, giving the fabric a rippled effect.

>> See pattern on page 48.

chevron eyelet skirt

This skirt evolved from a swatch shown in Barbara Walker's *Treasury of Knitting Patterns* with which she illustrates the difference between working a chevron eyelet pattern every row versus every other row. In my skirt, I have utilized both chevron patterns in tiers of three and worked in the round to avoid the inconvenience of working a chart on a wrong-side row. At the bottom of the skirt are the wider chevrons, which do not appear to make an eyelet pattern—the yarnovers become spaces in a ladder, rather than holes, once they are taken up by decreases in the following round. In the narrower, sharper set of chevrons, the yarnovers are knit on the following round and therefore form more rounded eyelets. The two patterns are syncopated in a pleasing way and serve as a lesson on the different rates of slope. One can also observe that the ladders of openwork on the every-row version are single strands whereas the ladders in the other version are two strands twined together. To accentuate the zigzag effect, I have added one last chevron element in a tiny scale—a picot edging that looks as if it were cut out with pinking shears.

>> See pattern on page 50.

interlocking squares pillow and bolster

Barbara Walker created a series of forty-two bias-knit squares containing geometric eyelet patterns in her *Fourth Treasury of Knitting Patterns*. In her book, Walker suggests several ways these eyelet charts might be used together in a sort of patchwork to form a bedspread, poncho, or skirt, and I've used this as a jumping-off point for the design presented here. Walker's Interlocking Squares are perfect for this home decorating project as the pattern is reminiscent of Chinese furniture—particularly the Chinese-style chair backs popular during the Art Deco period (and featured prominently in the contemporary line of furniture by West Elm). A single repeat forms a standard throw pillow cover, and a border in a darker shade frames the center pattern for a finished look. Three pattern repeats are worked in tandem from one corner on the bias to create a bolster cover for a body pillow insert. The bolster serves as a mock headboard on a full bed and would also look handsome along the back of a bench. The saturated colors and natural beauty of hemp yarn makes these pillows very special.

>> See pattern on page 52.

rose trellis blouse

This floral lace pattern is delineated with eyelets. It features a grid of rounded diamonds and stylized "rosebuds" at the intersection and in the center of each diamond. An oval represents the coiled petals of the rosebud, and an eyelet center represents the flower top. With its vaulted "trellis" framework, this rosebud arrangement has a Romanesque quality, reminiscent of a colonnade in a medieval cloister. I manipulated the trellis outline to form a front neck placket. When I was well into knitting this sweater—which is made in a yummy and very delicate cashmere silk yarn—I found a doppelganger of the pattern in the most curious place: on perforated fancy toilet tissue in a restroom. Apparently the patterns of the Victorian era are still used to connote domestic comfort today.

>> See pattern on page 55.

lace puff bloomers

I confess I have a near fetish for bloomers. In high school I bought poofy corduroy jodhpurs—the uniform of the Women's Land Army, a British volunteer corps during World Wars I and II—from an army surplus store, and these were my regular attire. When I traveled to Morocco I returned with a new favorite: *sousdi* harem pants. There are many versions of cropped, poofy pants for undergarments and outerwear, but Amelia Bloomer (the editor of the first American temperence newspaper for women, *The Lily*, which began in 1849) and the proponents of Victorian Dress Reform made them popular and the name stuck. These women advocated Middle Eastern-inspired wide pants with tapered cuffs, as they were a comfortable, respectable alternative to the voluminous long skirts of the day, and offered women new freedom and safety when bicycle riding. The designer Paul Poiret also tried to bring pants into womenswear, but the style did not take hold until the mid-twentieth century. These bloomers, designed for lounging around the house in luxury, are made with fine-gauge organic cotton and with silk ribbons woven through the eyelets at the waistband and cuffs.

>> *See pattern on page 58.*

celtic braid
eyelet wrap

The Celtic knotwork found in
scroll illuminations and metalwork has always been an inspiration for my knitted designs—
interweaving motifs are not only
adaptable to cabled designs, but
also to some unorthodox knitting
techniques, which I have used
here. The braided strips outlined
by eyelets on one end of this wrap
resemble the Braided Neckpiece
from my first book, *Loop-d-Loop*.
In that piece, rather than working
a complicated braided Aran cable,
I simply bound off and cast on to
form slits on one end, then made
knitted strips on the other end and
wove them through. For the lace
version of this wrap, I worked in
Garter stitch for reversibility. In
a linen and mohair blend yarn,
the wrap has structure and can
be arranged to form a hoodlike
collar.

>> See pattern on page 60.

top-down eyelet t-shirt

ABBREVIATIONS

Sk3p: Slip 1 st knitwise, k3tog (3 yos), pass slipped st over to decrease 3 sts.

YOKE

Using Long-Tail CO (see Special Techniques, page 154) and smaller needle for girl's sizes or larger needle for women's sizes, loosely CO 72 sts. Join for working in the rnd, being careful not to twist sts; pm for beginning of rnd.

Rnds 1-3: Knit.

Rnd 4: *K4, yo; repeat from * to end.

Rnd 5: *K4, slip 1 (yo from previous rnd), yo (there are now 2 yos in a row); repeat from * to end.

Rnd 6: *K4, slip 2 (yos from previous rnds), yo (there are now 3 yos in a row); repeat from * to end.

Rnd 7: *K4, k3tog (3 yos); repeat from * to end—90 sts.

Rnds 8-10: Knit.

Rnd 11: *K5, yo; repeat from * to end.

Rnd 12: *K5, slip 1, yo; repeat from * to end.

Rnd 13: *K5, slip 2, yo; repeat from * to end.

Rnd 14: *K5, k3tog; repeat from * to end—108 sts.

Rnds 15-17: Knit.

Rnd 18: *K6, yo; repeat from * to end.

Rnd 19: *K6, slip 1, yo; repeat from * to end.

Rnd 20: *K6, slip 2, yo; repeat from * to end.

SIZES

Girl's 4-5T (Girl's 6-8 years, Girl's 10-12 years, Women's Small, Women's Medium)

Note: The girl's sizes can be worn as a tunic or dress; the women's sizes can be worn as a T-shirt (or follow instructions below to work a tunic or dress length). If working the girl's sizes, use the smaller needle and the Girl's Version gauge; if working the women's sizes, be sure to use the larger needle and the Women's Version gauge.

FINISHED MEASUREMENTS

25 (28, 32, 31 1/2, 36)" bust

YARN

Girl's Version: Filatura Di Crosa Zara Chiné (100% merino wool; 136 yards / 50 grams): 4 (5, 6, –, –) balls #1771 Fuchsia

Women's Version: Filatura Di Crosa Zara (100% merino wool; 136 yards / 50 grams): – (–, –, 6, 6) balls #1741 Salmon.

Note: If you are working a longer length, you may need to purchase additional yarn.

NEEDLES

Girl's Version: One 24" (60 cm) long or longer circular (circ) needle size US 6 (4 mm)

Women's Version: One 24" (60 cm) long or longer circular (circ) needle size US 8 (5 mm)

Change needle size if necessary to obtain correct gauge.

NOTIONS

Stitch marker

GAUGE

Girl's Version: 18 sts and 26 rnds = 4" (10 cm) in Stockinette stitch (St st), using smaller needle

Women's Version: 16 sts and 24 rnds = 4" (10 cm) in Stockinette stitch (St st), using larger needle

Rnd 21: *K6, k3tog; repeat from * to end—126 sts.

Rnds 22-24: Knit.

Rnd 25: *K7, yo; repeat from * to end.

Rnd 26: *K7, slip 1, yo; repeat from * to end.

Rnd 27: *K7, slip 2, yo; repeat from * to end.

Rnd 28: *K7, k3tog; repeat from * to end—144 sts.

SIZES GIRL'S 6-8 YEARS, GIRL'S 10-12 YEARS, WOMEN'S SMALL, WOMEN'S MEDIUM ONLY

Rnds 29-31: Knit.

Rnd 32: *K8, yo; repeat from * to end.

Rnd 33: *K8, slip 1, yo; repeat from * to end.

Rnd 34: *K8, slip 2, yo; repeat from * to end.

Rnd 35: *K8, k3tog; repeat from * to end—162 sts.

ALL SIZES: Knit 1 rnd.

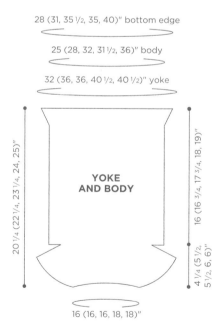

28 (31, 35 1/2, 35, 40)" bottom edge

25 (28, 32, 31 1/2, 36)" body

32 (36, 36, 40 1/2, 40 1/2)" yoke

YOKE AND BODY

20 1/4 (22 1/4, 23 1/4, 24, 25)"

16 (16, 16, 17 3/4, 18, 19)"

4 1/4 (5 1/2, 5 1/2, 6, 6)"

16 (16, 16, 18, 18)"

Note: Piece is worked from the top down.

BODY

Divide Sleeves and Body: K8 (9, 9, 9, 9), BO 24 (27, 27, 27, 27) sts for Sleeve, k48 (54, 54, 54, 54), BO 24 (27, 27, 27, 27) sts for Sleeve, k40 (45, 45, 45, 45). *Note: Beginning of rnd marker is now at back right shoulder.*

Next Rnd: K8 (9, 9, 9, 9), CO 8, (9, 18, 9, 18) sts for underarm, k48 (54, 54, 54, 54), CO 8 (9, 18, 9, 18) sts for underarm, knit to end—112 (126, 144, 126, 144) sts.

Rnd 1: *K8 (9, 9, 9, 9), yo; repeat from * to end.

Rnd 2: *K8 (9, 9, 9, 9), slip 1, yo; repeat from * to end.

Rnd 3: *K8 (9, 9, 9, 9), slip 2, yo; repeat from * to end.

Rnd 4: *K7 (8, 8, 8, 8), sk3p; repeat from * to end.

Rnds 5-7: Knit.

Repeat Rnds 1-7 until piece measures approximately 14 1/4 (15, 16, 16, 17) from underarm, or to 1 3/4 (1 3/4, 1 3/4, 2, 2)" less than desired length, ending with Rnd 7. *Note: If you prefer a more A-line shape in the Girl's Version, begin the following Shape Hem section at the point at which you want the shaping to begin, and work as indicated in the note below that section. If you want to work a tunic or dress for the Women's Version, begin the Shape Hem section at the hip, and work as indicated in the note below that section. If you choose to work a longer length, remember to purchase additional yarn.*

Shape Hem

Rnd 1: *K8 (9, 9, 9, 9), yo; repeat from * to end.

Rnd 2: *K8 (9, 9, 9, 9), slip 1, yo; repeat from * to end.

Rnd 3: *K8 (9, 9, 9, 9), slip 2, yo; repeat from * to end.

Rnd 4: *K8 (9, 9, 9, 9), k3tog; repeat from * to end—126 (140, 160, 140, 160) sts.

Rnds 5-7: Knit.

Rnd 8: *K9 (10, 10, 10, 10), yo; repeat from * to end.

Three rows of yarnover strands are taken up at once and worked into the stitch to the top right of the eyelet, causing a rippled effect in the fabric.

Rnd 9: *K9 (10, 10, 10, 10), slip 1, yo; repeat from * to end.

Rnd 10: *K9 (10, 10, 10, 10), slip 2, yo; repeat from * to end.

Rnd 11: *K8 (9, 9, 9, 9), sk3p; repeat from * to end.

Rnd 12: Knit. BO all sts.

Note: Rnd 4 increases each repeat by 1 st and Rnd 11 returns each repeat back to the st count you had at the end of Rnd 4. If you are working additional shaping, work Rnds 1-7 once, then continue working Rnds 1-7, working 1 additional st before the yo on every repeat of Rnd 1. When you reach the desired circumference, work Rnds 8-12, working 1 additional st before the yo on Rnd 8. If you want to work even for a while before binding off, work 2 additional knit rnds (Rnds 13 and 14), then repeat Rnds 1-14 until you reach your desired length, ending with Rnd 12 on the final repeat.

FINISHING
Block lightly with steam.

chevron eyelet skirt

STITCH PATTERN
1x1 Rib
(multiple of 2 sts; 1-rnd repeat)

All Rnds: *K1, p1; repeat from * to end.

SKIRT
Using larger circ needle and Provisional CO (see Special Techniques, page 154), CO 141 (161, 181, 201, 221, 241) sts.

Row 1 (RS): Knit.

Row 2: Purl.

Row 3 (Turning Row): *P2tog, yo; repeat from * to last st, p1.

Row 4: P1, *k1, p1; repeat from * to end.

Row 5: Unravel Provisional CO. Fold hem to WS. K2tog (1 st on needle together with 1 st from CO), *p2tog (1 st on needle together with 1 st from CO), k2tog (1 st on needle together with 1 st from CO); repeat from * to end. Do not turn.

Next Rnd: Join for working in the rnd; pm for beginning of rnd. Begin 1x1 Rib, decrease 1 st at end of rnd—140 (160, 180, 200, 220, 240) sts remain. Work even for 2 rnds. Knit 2 rnds.

Next Rnd: Change to Wide Chevron from Chart; work even until 3 vertical repeats of Chart have been completed. Change to Narrow Chevron from Chart; work even until 3 vertical repeats of Chart have been completed. Change to St st (knit every rnd); work even until piece measures 15 (14 1/2, 15, 14, 14, 13 1/2)" from the beginning, ending 5 (0, 5, 0, 5, 0) sts past beginning of rnd marker. Reposition marker if necessary for new beginning of rnd. Place second marker 70 (80, 90, 100, 110, 120) sts after first marker.

Shape Hips: Decrease 4 sts this rnd, then every 5 (5, 4, 4, 4, 4) rnds 2 (3, 4, 5, 6, 7) times, as follows: [K2tog, knit to 2 sts before marker, ssk] twice—128 (144, 160, 176, 192, 208) sts remain. Work even until piece measures 18 (18, 18 1/2, 18 1/2, 19, 19)" from the beginning.

Next Rnd: Change to 1x1 Rib. Work even for 1 rnd.

Establish Pocket Openings: Continuing in rib, work 10 (14, 16, 16, 20, 24) sts, BO next 14 (14, 14, 16, 16, 16) sts, work 15 (15, 19, 23, 23, 23) sts (not including 1 st left on right-hand needle after BOs), BO next 14 (14, 14, 16, 16, 16) sts, work to end. Work even for 1 rnd, CO 14 (14, 14, 16, 16, 16) sts over BO sts. Work even until piece measures 1 1/2" from beginning of ribbing. Change to smaller needle. Work even until piece measures 3" from beginning of ribbing. BO all sts in pattern.

FINISHING

Pocket Ribbing (make 2): Using larger needle and Provisional CO, CO 15 (15, 15, 17, 17, 17) sts. Work as for Skirt hem through Row 5; turn. Work 2 rows in 1x1 Rib as established. BO all sts in pattern.

Block as desired. Sew side edges of Skirt and Pocket Ribbing.

Skirt Lining: Cut 2 pieces of lining fabric using Skirt as template, leaving 1/2" seam allowance on sides, 1 1/2" allowance at top for waistband, and cutting piece to same length as Skirt on bottom edge. Sew sides, using 1/2" seam allowance. Fold top edge 1/4" over to WS and press. Fold again 1 1/4" to WS and press. Insert elastic into fold and sew casing closed. Fold bottom edge 1/2" to WS and press. Fold again 1" to WS and press. Sew bottom edge, making sure to secure both folds. With WSs of Skirt and lining together, sew top edge of lining just below top of Waistband.

Pocket Lining: Cut 2 pieces of lining fabric 4 1/2" wide x 9" long. Fold piece in half lengthwise, with RSs together. Sew side edges, using 1/2" seam allowance. Fold Top edge 1/2" to WS and press. Sew front edge of lining to BO edge of pocket opening and back edge of lining to CO edge of pocket opening. Sew Pocket Ribbing to BO edges of pocket openings, with picots facing down.

The Wide Chevron stitch pattern (shown on bottom) features open ladders of single strands while the Narrow Chevron stitch pattern (shown on top) features diagonal eyelets.

WIDE CHEVRON

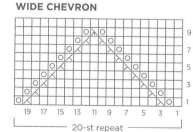

20-st repeat

10-rnd repeat

NARROW CHEVRON

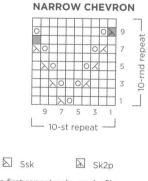

10-st repeat

10-rnd repeat

KEY

☐ Knit   ☐ Yo   ☒ K2tog   ☒ Ssk   ☒ Sk2p

▨ On last repeat only, omit this st; it will be worked as part of sk2p at beginning of Rnd 9.

▨ On first repeat only, work s2kp over last st of previous rnd and first 2 sts of current rnd.

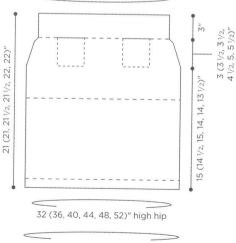

30 (34, 37 3/4, 41 1/2, 45 1/4, 49)" waist

21 (21, 21 1/2, 21 1/2, 22, 22)"

3"

3 (3 1/2, 3 1/2, 4 1/2, 5, 5 1/2)"

15 (14 1/2, 15, 14, 14, 13 1/2)"

32 (36, 40, 44, 48, 52)" high hip

35 (40, 45, 50, 55, 60)" bottom edge

interlocking squares pillow and bolster

Throw Pillow

FRONT

Using MC, CO 3 sts. Purl 1 row.

Next Row (RS): Begin Interlocking Squares Pattern from Chart; work even, through Row 146 of Chart, working increases and decreases as indicated in Chart—1 st remains. Fasten off.

FINISHING

Border: With RS facing, using circ needle and A, [pick up and knit 60 sts along side edge, pm] 4 times—240 sts. Join for working in the rnd.

Rnd 1: Knit.

Rnd 2: [K1-f/b, knit to 1 st before marker, k1-f/b] 4 times—248 sts.

Repeat Rnds 1 and 2 three times—272 sts. BO all sts knitwise.

Block piece.

BACK

Cut fabric for Back using Front as a template, and leaving ⁵/₈" seam allowance around all edges. You may wish to take care to align any pattern repeat in fabric if using a printed design. Fold seam allowance to WS of fabric and press. With WSs of

FINISHED MEASUREMENTS

Throw Pillow: 18" x 18"

Bolster: Approximately 18" wide x 54" long

YARN

Throw Pillow: Lanaknits Allhemp6 (100% hemp; 100 grams / 165 yards): 2 hanks #19 Sprout (MC); 1 hank #20 Avocado (A)

Bolster: Lanaknits Allhemp6 (100% hemp; 100 grams / 165 yards): 5 hanks #19 Sprout (MC); 1 hank #20 Avocado (A)

NEEDLES

One pair size US 7 (4.5 mm) needles

One 36" (90 cm) long circular (circ) needle size US 7 (4.5 mm)

Change needle size if necessary to obtain correct gauge.

NOTIONS

Throw Pillow: Stitch markers; 18" square pillow form; 18" square pillow cover in coordinating solid color (optional); ³/₄ yard fabric for back of Pillow; sewing needle and matching sewing thread

Bolster: Stitch markers; 20" x 54" body pillow form (finished Bolster will stretch to fit pillow form); 20" x 54" body pillow cover in coordinating solid color (optional); 2 ¹/₂ yards fabric for back of Bolster; sewing needle and matching sewing thread

Note: Since pillow forms are usually white, a coordinating cover will provide a more attractive background to show through the lace of the pillow.

GAUGE

16 sts and 24 rows = 4" (10 cm) in Stockinette stitch (St st)

Front and Back together, using sewing needle and thread, sew 3 sides together, catching the edge st of the Front and the pressed fold of the Back. Insert pillow form and sew fourth side closed.

Bolster

NOTE: The Diamonds are shaped by working increases along the lower edges, and decreases along the upper edges. Each successive Diamond is worked off the upper left-hand edge of the preceding Diamond. The Second Diamond is worked off the upper left-hand edge of the First Diamond, and is started when you begin working the upper edge decreases for the First Diamond. The Third Diamond is worked in a similar manner off the Second Diamond.

FRONT

First Diamond: Using MC, CO 3 sts. Purl 1 row.

(RS) Begin Interlocking Squares Pattern from Chart; work even, through Row 72 of Chart, working increases and decreases as indicated in Chart—75 sts.

Begin Second Diamond (RS): Work Row 73 to last 2 sts, place marker (pm) for beginning of Second Diamond, work Row 1 to end, omitting sts and working increases as indicated in Chart. Continuing to work Diamonds separately on either side of marker, work even through Row 144 of First Diamond, and Row 72 of Second Diamond.

Begin Third Diamond (RS): Work Row 145 of First Diamond, removing marker, then Row 73 of Second Diamond to last 2 sts, pm for beginning of Third Diamond, work Row 1 to end, omitting sts and working increases as indicated in Chart. Work even through Row 145 of Second Diamond, removing marker. Work even on Third Diamond only until Chart is complete. Fasten off.

FINISHING

Border: With RS facing, using A, pick up and knit 60 sts along one short side edge.

Row 1 (WS): Knit.

Row 2: K1-f/b, knit to last st, k1-f/b—62 sts.

Repeat Rows 1 and 2 three times—68 sts. BO all sts knitwise.

Work Border for remaining short side.

With RS facing, using A, pick up and knit 170 sts along one long side edge. Work as for short side Borders—178 sts. Work Border for remaining long side. Sew Borders at corners. Block piece.

BACK

Work as for Throw Pillow.

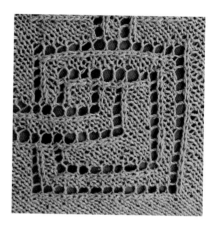

This stitch pattern is worked on the bias from the bottom right corner, so the shapes created in the pattern are diamonds as you work them. The base of each diamond is formed by new stitches above the eyelets, and thus has no hard outline. The tops of each diamond, however, have outlines formed by decreases that create the illusion of interlocking shapes.

INTERLOCKING SQUARES PATTERN

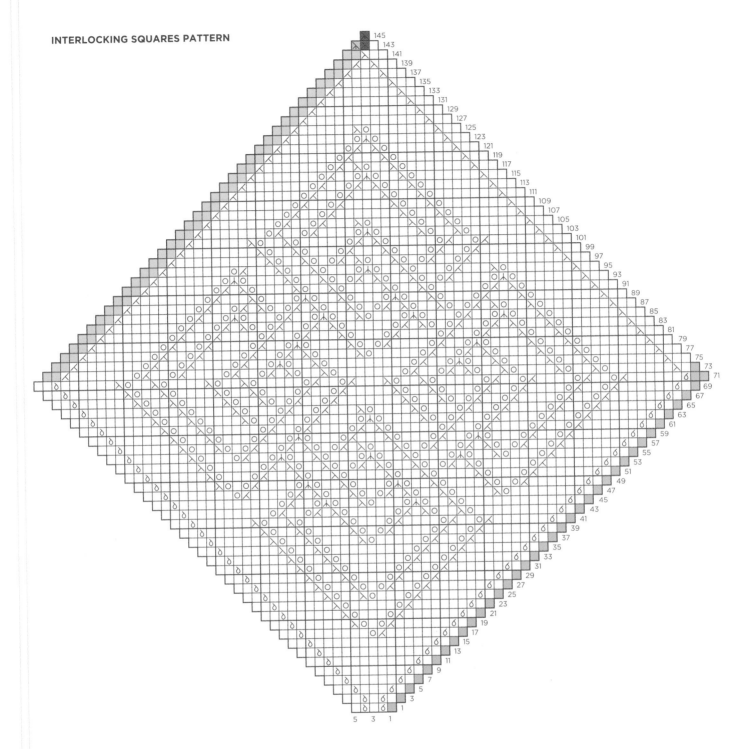

KEY

Note: Chart shows only RS rows. Purl all sts on WS rows.

☐	Knit
⟨6⟩	M1-r
⟨δ⟩	M1-l
☐	Yo
⟨⟩	K2tog
⟨⟩	Ssk
⟨⟩	Sk2p
⟨⟩	S2kp2

Omit these sts when working the top left-hand edge of the First and Second Diamonds of the Bolster; work these sts as knit sts when working the Throw Pillow and the top left-hand edge of the Third Diamond of the Bolster.

Omit these sts when working the lower right-hand edge of the Second and Third Diamonds of the Bolster; work these sts as knit sts when working the Throw Pillow and the lower right-hand edge of the First Diamond of the Bolster.

Omit this st when working the lower right-hand edge of the Second and Third Diamonds of the Bolster; work this st as shown when working the Throw Pillow and the lower right-hand edge of the First Diamond of the Bolster.

Work this st as a knit st when working the First and Second Diamonds of the Bolster; work st as shown when working the Throw Pillow and the Third Diamond of the Bolster.

Work this st as shown when working First and Second Diamonds of the Bolster; work as a knit st when working the Throw Pillow and the Third Diamond of the Bolster.

rose trellis blouse

SIZES

X-Small/Small (Medium/Large, Large/X-Large, 2X/3X-Large, 4X/5X-Large)

To fit bust sizes 30-34 (36-40, 42-48, 50-54, 56-60) *Note: If you want a closer-fitting garment, work a size where the upper measurement of the range fits your measurements. If you want a looser-fitting garment, work a size where the lower measurement fits your measurements.*

FINISHED MEASUREMENTS

33 1/2 (40, 46 1/2, 53, 59 1/2)" bust

YARN

Filatura Di Crosa Superior (70% cashmere / 30% schappé silk; 330 yards / 25 grams): 3 (4, 4, 5, 6) balls #27 Steel Grey

NEEDLES

One pair straight needles size US 2 (2.75 mm)

Change needle size if necessary to obtain correct gauge.

NOTIONS

Stitch markers

GAUGE

20 sts = 3 1/4" (8.5 cm) and 44 rows = 4 3/4" (12 cm) in Rose Trellis Pattern from Chart

24 sts and 40 rows = 4" (10 cm) in Reverse Stockinette stitch (Rev St st)

SHAPING NOTE

When working shaping for the armholes, neck, and sleeve cap, make sure to keep the Rose Trellis Pattern correct. In other words, if you cannot work a full decrease within the Rose Trellis Pattern (after working the shaping decreases), do not work the yo(s) associated with that decrease in the pattern, and vice versa; work the sts in St st instead.

BACK

CO 103 (123, 143, 163, 183) sts. Purl 1 row.

(RS) P0 (10, 0, 10, 0), pm if desired, work Rose Trellis Pattern from Chart (working repeats as indicated for your size) to last 0 (10, 0, 10, 0) sts, pm if desired, purl to end. Working first and last 0 (10, 0, 10, 0) sts of every row in Rev St st, work Rows 1-44 of Chart three times, then work Rows 1-4 (4, 8, 8, 12) once.

Shape Armholes (RS): Continuing with Chart, work Rows 5 (5, 9, 9, 13)-44 once, then Rows 1-44 for the remainder of the Back and AT THE SAME TIME, BO 0 (6, 9, 15, 17) sts at beginning of next 2 rows, 2 sts at beginning of next 0 (0, 0, 4, 10) rows, then decrease 1 st each side every other row 5 (9, 11, 11, 8) times (see Shaping Note)—93 (93, 103, 103, 113) sts remain. Work even until armhole measures 8 (8 1/2, 9, 9 1/2, 10)", ending with a WS row. BO all sts loosely.

FRONT

Work as for Back until Rows 1-44 of Rose Trellis Pattern have been worked twice. Work Rows 45-82 of Chart once, then work Rows 83-126 once and AT THE SAME TIME, when piece measures same as for Back to armhole shaping, shape armholes as for Back—93 (93, 103, 103, 113) sts

ROSE TRELLIS PATTERN

KEY

☐ Knit on RS, purl on WS.	◯ Yo	⟋ Ssk	⟋ K3tog
⊡ Purl on RS, knit on WS.	⟍ K2tog	⟑ Sk2p	▨ No stitch

remain. Work Rows 83-126 (completing armhole shaping for largest size) until armhole measures 6 (6 1/2, 7, 7 1/2, 8)", ending with a WS row.

Shape Neck (RS): Work 37 (37, 42, 42, 47) sts, join a second ball of yarn, bind off center 19 sts, work to end. Working both sides at the same time, decrease 1 st each neck edge every row 18 times—19 (19, 24, 24, 29) sts remain each side for shoulders. Work even until armhole measures same as for Back. BO all sts.

SLEEVES

Cast on 90 (96, 102, 108, 114) sts. Begin Rev St st; work even until piece measures 4 (4, 4 1/2, 4 1/2, 5)" from the beginning, ending with a WS row.

Shape Cap (RS): BO 0 (6, 9, 15, 17) sts at beginning of next 2 rows, decrease 1 st every 4 rows 0 (6, 8, 12, 13) times, every other row 20 (10, 7, 3, 3) times, then every row 6 (6, 6, 2, 2) times. BO remaining 38 (40, 42, 44, 44) sts.

FINISHING

Block as desired. Sew shoulder seams. Set in Sleeves. Sew side and Sleeve seams.

WAISTBAND

CO 10 (10, 12, 12, 14) sts. Begin Garter st (knit every row); work even until piece mesures 31 1/2 (38, 44 1/2, 51, 57 1/2)" from the beginning, unstretched. BO all sts. Beginning at left side seam, sew Waistband to bottom edge of Blouse.

The rosebud motif (with four buds at each center and one at each intersection of the tiled pattern) is depicted by a solid oval area crowned with a single eyelet. This lone eyelet denotes the slightly opened top of the bud, and a gathering decrease slightly above suggests the enfolded petals.

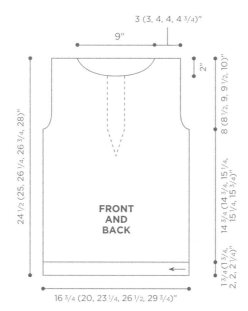

3 (3, 4, 4, 4 3/4)"

9"

2"

8 (8 1/2, 9, 9 1/2, 10)"

24 1/2 (25, 26 1/4, 26 3/4, 28)"

FRONT AND BACK

14 3/4 (14 3/4, 15 1/4, 15 1/4, 15 3/4)"

1 3/4 (1 3/4, 2, 2, 2 1/4)"

16 3/4 (20, 23 1/4, 26 1/2, 29 3/4)"

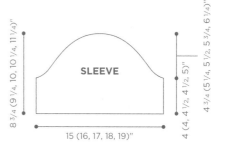

SLEEVE

8 3/4 (9 1/4, 10, 10 1/4, 11 1/4)"

4 3/4 (5 1/4, 5 1/2, 5 3/4, 6 1/4)"

4 (4, 4 1/2, 4 1/2, 5)"

15 (16, 17, 18, 19)"

lace puff bloomers

STITCH PATTERNS

Eyelet Pattern

(odd number of sts; 6-row repeat)

Row 1 (RS): Purl.

Row 2: P1, *yo, p2tog; repeat from * to end.

Rows 3 and 5: Purl.

Rows 4 and 6: Knit.

Repeat Rows 1-6 for Eyelet Pattern.

Lace Puff Pattern

(multiple varies; 12-row repeat)

Row 1 (RS): K3, *yo, p1, yo, k3; repeat from * to end.

Row 2 and all WS Rows: Purl.

Row 3: K4, yo, p1, yo, *k5, yo, p1, yo; repeat from * to last 4 sts, knit to end.

Row 5: K5, yo, p1, yo, *k7, yo, p1, yo; repeat from * to last 5 sts, knit to end.

Row 7: K6, yo, p1, yo, *k9, yo, p1, yo; repeat from * to last 6 sts, knit to end.

Row 9: K3, *k4tog-tbl, p1, k4tog, k3; repeat from * to end.

Row 11: K3, *p3tog, k3; repeat from * to end.

Row 12: Purl.

Repeat Rows 1-12 for Lace Puff Pattern.

LEGS (both alike)

Using Provisional CO (see Special Techniques, page 154), CO 111 (119, 127, 135, 143) sts. Begin St st, beginning with a purl row; work even for 3 rows.

Turning Row (RS): *P2tog, yo; repeat from * to last st, p1. Work even in St st for 3 rows.

(RS) Unravel Provisional CO. *K2tog (1 st on needle together with 1 st from CO); repeat from * to end. Purl 1 row.

(RS) Change to Eyelet Pattern; work even for 12 rows.

(RS) Change to Lace Puff Pattern; work Rows 1-12 twice, then Rows 1-10 once.

SIZES

Small (Medium, Large, X-Large, 2X-Large)

FINISHED MEASUREMENTS

34 (37, 40 1/2, 43 1/2, 46 1/2)" hip

28 1/2 (31 1/2, 35, 38, 41)" waist

28 1/2 (28 1/2, 29 1/2, 29 1/2, 30 1/2)" long, including finished waistband

21" inseam; *Note: Instructions are included to adjust*

inseam length if desired. If you increase the inseam length, you may need to purchase additional yarn.

YARN

Rowan Purelife Organic Cotton 4-ply (100% organic cotton; 180 yards / 50 grams): 8 (9, 10, 11, 12) skeins #759 Oak Bark

NEEDLES

One pair size US 4 (3.5 mm) needles

Change needle size if necessary to obtain correct gauge.

NOTIONS

Waste yarn; stitch markers; 1 yard 3/8" wide elastic; sewing needle and sewing thread; 3 yards 1/2" wide ribbon (optional)

GAUGE

26 sts and 36 rows = 4" (10 cm) in Stockinette stitch (St st)

(RS) K3, *p3tog, but do not drop sts from left-hand needle, insert tip of right-hand needle into back of second st on left-hand needle and knit it, slip sts from left-hand needle, k3; repeat from * to last st, k1-f/b—139 (149, 159, 169, 179) sts. Purl 1 row.

(RS) Change to St st; work even until piece measures 8" from bottom edge, ending with a WS row. *Note: The inseam will measure 21" when finished. If you wish to adjust the inseam length, do so now before beginning inseam shaping. Remember that if you add length, you may need to purchase additional yarn.*

Shape Inseam (RS): Increase 1 st each side this row, then every 10 rows 7 times—155 (165, 175, 185, 195) sts. Work even until piece measures 21" from bottom edge, ending with a WS row.

Shape Crotch (RS): BO 14 sts at beginning of next 2 rows, decrease 1 st each side every row 4 (3, 2, 1, 0) time(s), then every other row 4 (5, 6, 7, 8) times—111 (121, 131, 141, 151) sts remain. Work even until crotch measures 3", ending with a WS row.

Shape Hip (RS): K53 (58, 63, 68, 73), ssk, pm, k1, k2tog, knit to end—109

(119, 129, 139, 149) sts remain. Work even for 3 rows.

Decrease Row (RS): Decrease 2 sts this row, every 4 rows 4 (4, 5, 5, 5) times, then every other row 3 (3, 2, 2, 2) times, as follows: Knit to 2 sts before marker, ssk, sm, k1, k2tog, knit to end—93 (103, 113, 123, 133) sts. Work even until crotch measures 6 (6, 7, 7, 8)", ending with a WS row.

(RS) Change to Eyelet Pattern; work even for 12 rows. Change to St st; work even for 2 rows.

Turning Row (RS): *P2tog, yo; repeat from * to last st, p1. Work even in St st for 4 rows. BO all sts purlwise.

FINISHING

Block pieces lightly. Sew inseams. Sew Legs together at crotch. Fold waistband over elastic to WS at turning row, and sew to WS, being careful not to let sts show on RS, leaving opening at back seam, and leaving elastic ends out at back to adjust fit. Try on Bloomers and adjust elastic to fit comfortably. Sew elastic ends together. Sew back waistband seam.

Thread ribbon through eyelets at waist and Leg cuffs (optional).

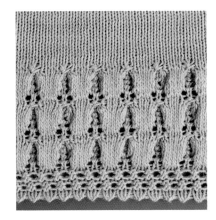

A quilted effect results when yarnovers create extra volume at each side of the lace motif, and each solid Stockinette stitch "puff" is then reduced at its corners.

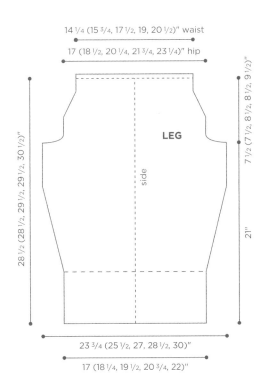

14 1/4 (15 3/4, 17 1/2, 19, 20 1/2)" waist

17 (18 1/2, 20 1/4, 21 3/4, 23 1/4)" hip

7 1/2 (7 1/2, 8 1/2, 8 1/2, 9 1/2)"

LEG

side

21"

28 1/2 (28 1/2, 29 1/2, 29 1/2, 30 1/2)"

23 3/4 (25 1/2, 27, 28 1/2, 30)"

17 (18 1/4, 19 1/2, 20 3/4, 22)"

celtic braid eyelet wrap

SIZES
Small (Medium, Large,
X-Large, 2X-Large)

**FINISHED
MEASUREMENTS**
14 1/4" wide x 44 (48, 52, 56,
60)" long

YARN
Louet KidLin Light Worsted
Weight (53% kid mohair /
24% linen / 23% nylon; 120
yards / 50 grams): 4 (4, 4, 5,
5) hanks #62 Orange Berry

NEEDLES
One pair size US 6 (4 mm)
needles

Change needle size
if necessary to obtain
correct gauge.

GAUGE
16 sts and 29 rows = 4"
(10 cm) in Garter stitch

WRAP

CO 27 sts.

Shape Wrap (RS): Increase 1 st at beginning of this row, then every row 9 times, as follows: K2, yo, knit to end—37 sts.

Begin Chart

Row 1 (RS): K2, yo, work across 33 sts of Celtic Braid Pattern from Chart, knit to end—38 sts.

Row 2: K2, yo, knit to end—39 sts.

Row 3: K2, yo, work across 35 sts from Chart, knit to end—40 sts.

Row 4: K2, yo, knit to end—41 sts.

Row 5: K2, yo, pm, work across 37 sts from Chart, pm, knit to end—42 sts.

Row 6: K2, yo, knit to end—43 sts.

Row 7: K2, yo, knit to marker, sm, work Chart to next marker, sm, knit to end—44 sts.

Row 8: K2, yo, knit to end—45 sts.

Rows 9-20: Repeat Rows 7 and 8—57 sts.

Row 21: K2, yo, k2tog, work to end.

Rows 22-69: Repeat Row 21. Chart should be complete.

Row 70: K2, yo, k2tog, knit to end.

Repeat Row 70 until piece measures 44 (48, 52, 56, 60)", or to desired length from the beginning, ending with a WS Row. BO all sts.

FINISHING

Block piece lightly.

CELTIC BRAID PATTERN

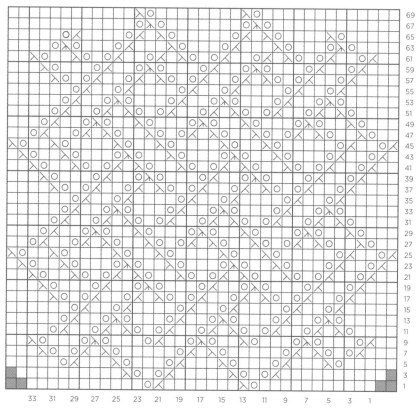

The fuzziness of the kid mohair in the yarn softens the graphic, diagonal outlines of the Celtic Braid Pattern.

KEY

Note: Chart shows only RS rows.
Knit all sts on WS rows.

	Knit		Ssk
○	Yo		Sk2p
	K2tog		No stitch

SAMPLERS

Arrangements and Pairings

IN THIS CHAPTER I PRESENT PROJECTS THAT PAY HOMAGE TO THE sampler, a form that is closely bound with the history of lace knitting. The modern knitter can be notoriously impatient when it comes to swatching, which is why most publishers print a warning next to the recommended needles for a project (e.g., "change needle size if necessary to obtain correct gauge"). All too often this necessary part of the knitting process is skipped over, sometimes with disastrous results. Imagine then, the amazing feat of knitters from the past who created swatch samplers of mind-boggling size and diversity. Either worked in a continuous strip that was rolled up and stored, or preserved between the pages of large albums, samplers served as a visual record of stitch patterns that were passed down from relatives or perhaps a visiting neighbor.

During the Industrial Revolution, the purpose of swatch samplers transformed from a necessary way to record stitch patterns to a purely decorative device. The advent of mass publishing coincided with the rising middle-class Victorians' newfound taste for lace and ornament, and the ladies magazines published patterns for all sorts of handwork. Because of this, knitting as a hobby grew alongside other crafts, such as bobbin lace, tatting, embroidery, and crochet. These publications documented stitch patterns that had previously been passed on through sampler knitting, and so the sampler was used instead as a decorative element in knit design. Each project in this chapter is essentially a sampler, from the straightforward lace patterns separated by a raised line of stitches in the Milanese Shower Bolero on page 76, to the combination of stitches worked into the Shetland Shawl Dress on page 87.

As a designer, I always find it an interesting process to select stitches to combine in the same piece. Like motifs in classical music, lace stitches work well together in combination. They often appear to interrelate, to be developed along the same principle, or to be variations of each other at a different scale. Swatching is one of a knit designer's most powerful tools. When looking at a stitch pattern I seek a narrative of sorts to find out what mood or rhythm, time or place, it may evoke. Later, when I'm through working with a swatch, my daughter often commandeers the small piece to use as part of a doll costume or to sew a softie toy. I suppose this is her form of sampler.

smocked border triangle shawl

In Elizabeth Gaskell's novel *Cranford*, which is set in an 1830s country village in England, several genteel women of reduced means are knitting lace shawls out of wool mail-ordered from the Shetland Isles.

Fast-forward 180 years to an article for the online magazine *Twist Collective* in which Kate Davies explores the life of one of the first knitting entrepreneurs, Jane Gaugain, a mid-nineteenth–century knitting book author and shop owner in Edinburgh, Scotland. By unearthing various clues, Kate surmises that Gaskell's heroines may have ordered their materials from Jane. I get such a thrill when my love of knitting and literature intersect. The design here—a triangle shawl in Shetland wool—is my homage to Kate, Jane, and Elizabeth (and also to Judi Dench, who was brilliant in Masterpiece Theatre's Cranford series).

The shawl begins at the bottom tip. A smocked lace pattern forms a border, expanding up the edges as new repeats of a second pattern with a stacked diamond motif are brought into the center. The diamonds at the top of the triangle transition back to the smocked pattern, then scallop outward with a flourish, creating a ruffled edge that serves as a collar when worn.

>> See pattern on page 74.

milanese shower bolero

This compact, flirty little jacket is a study of stitch patterns with cascading lines. In the Shower Stitch pattern featured on the lower bodice, fountains of stitches sprout up out of centered open spaces; very few knit patterns flaunt such dramatic cutouts and arches. I also love the strong diagonal arched waves of the Milanese Stitch pattern I used on the lower sleeve. The Wing Stitch pattern featured on the upper bodice is only a single wing—I found a pattern of paired wings and left off its match to achieve a spiral effect. To create the ruffled front bands and collar I made up a variation of Bear Track lace; placing increases opposite the "claw" makes the chevron fabric edge buckle.

>> See pattern on page 76.

tiger and snail folkloric blouse

In bold red, this peasant blouse flaunts the spicier side of lace. For inspiration, I drew from the style of Eastern European folkloric dance costumes, and adorned the garment with a sampler of animal-inspired lace stitches. The Tiger Eye pattern actually reminds me of owls more than tigers; stacked up the center of this pullover, they appear like horseshoe cables with big round eyes. To complement the main body stitch pattern, I chose a side-to-side edging with a snail shell theme. Across the hem, the snail shells spiral in a manner that looks like a twined cable. So I thought it fitting to add some actual cable work, with lacy cables running up each sleeve and around the neck as ruching.

>> *See pattern on page 79.*

shetland twins capelet

The Shetland Twins are lozenge shaped medallions that frame distinct filling motifs—one a triad of vertical diamonds and the other more of a tic-tac-toe grid. In pictures of historic Shetland shawls, one can find many different fillers used for the medallion centers, and often a string of the pattern is sandwiched between rows of pine motif in the shawl's center square. To me, the lozenge motifs seem to be an openwork translation of the colorwork medallions found in Fair Isle knitting. Here I've used the twin lozenges on a larger scale in a rustic shawl-collared capelet done in Donegal tweed.

>> See pattern on page 82.

chevron and diamond jacket

This dramatic layering piece samples a few lace patterns magnified at a large scale. A quick knit in chunky merino, it is worked in one piece from the top down. The Chevron Feather on the center front placket reminds me of the interior of a magnificent Art Deco theater, with entranceways bordered in stylized palm fronds. In lace knitting, "feathering" means to decrease in opposition to the knit stitch grain so that a visible ridge is created and groups of stitches appear to travel on different directional planes. A Trellis Diamond pattern makes for a theatrical back. I used short rows to give a cutaway shape to the front waist so this cozy, layering piece is reminiscent of an usher's or bellhop's uniform jacket.

>> See pattern on page 84.

shetland shawl dress

Rather than create a traditional shawl for this book, I wanted to present one in a novel form. This dress was my solution. The skirt of the dress is essentially a shawl with a Shetland Twins motif in the center. Then the frame is worked outward and the "shawl" is made to dip down as the bodice is worked on the bias in a variety of lace stitches. A traditional lace edging adds flounce to the hem and thin spaghetti straps create a delicate neckline. As with a Shetland shawl, the juxtaposition of the various stitches works towards an overall effect. The bias drape sets off all the square and diamond shapes, echoing a frame within a frame, and the undulating waves of pattern repeat are like a sky punctuated by small eyelet stars. Crisp linen yarn lends strength to the fabric, but it would also be gorgeous in laceweight wool or a wool/silk blend.

>> See pattern on page 87.

smocked border triangle shawl

SHAWL

CO 7 sts. Begin pattern from Shawl Pattern Chart. Work through st 6, then work in reverse, beginning with st 3 and working back to st 1, reversing all sts except for p3togs. Work even until you have 18 (20, 22, 24) diamonds along right-hand edge and across row, working pattern repeats as indicated, and ending with Row 66 of Chart—195 (215, 235, 255) sts. Work Rows 67-85 of Chart, working pattern repeat as indicated—343 (375, 407, 439) sts. BO all sts purlwise.

FINISHING

Block, pinning top edge and sides between wraps to emphasize scalloping. Use starch (optional) along top 3" to stiffen top edge. You may also run a strand of invisible thread (optional) along base row of scalloping (Row 78 of Chart) to support ruffle.

SIZES

54 1/4 (59 3/4, 65, 70 1/4)" wide x 24 (26, 28 1/4, 30 1/4)" long

YARN

Jamieson & Smith Shetland 2-ply Jumper Weight (100% Shetland wool; 130 yards / 25 grams): 5 (5, 6, 7) skeins #29

NEEDLES

One 29" (70 cm) long or longer circular (circ) needle size US 7 (4.5 mm)

Change needle size if necessary to obtain correct gauge.

NOTIONS

Stitch markers; blocking pins; starch (optional); 1 spool invisible thread (optional)

GAUGE

15 sts and 22 1/2 rows = 4" (10 cm) in main pattern (outlined in red) from Shawl Pattern Chart

Diamonds in a half-drop arrangement expand by a half-repeat at each edge to accommodate one additional diamond on every tier.

SHAWL PATTERN

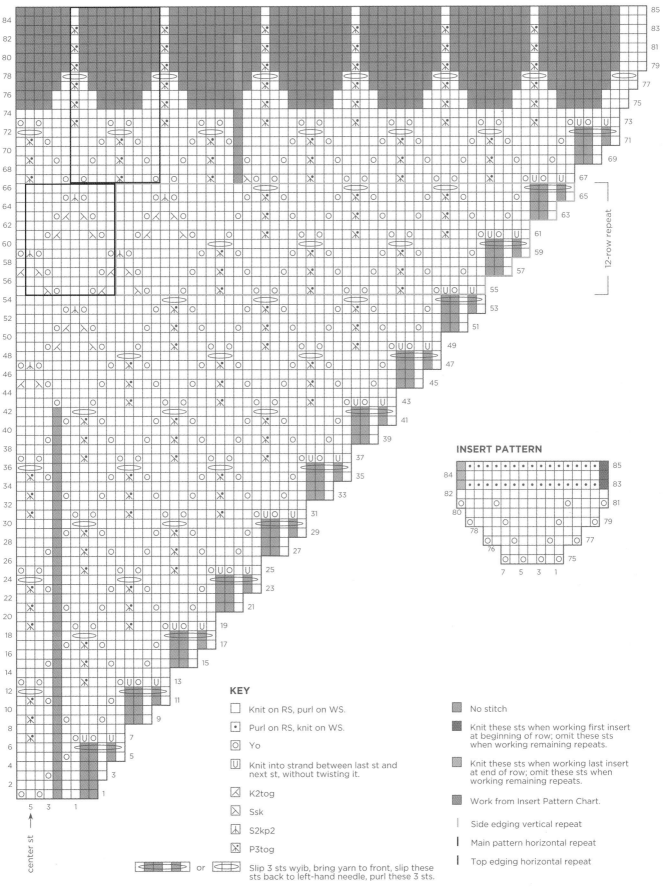

KEY

☐	Knit on RS, purl on WS.
⊡	Purl on RS, knit on WS.
⊙	Yo
⊍	Knit into strand between last st and next st, without twisting it.
╱	K2tog
╲	Ssk
⋏	S2kp2
⊠	P3tog

⬭ or ⬭ Slip 3 sts wyib, bring yarn to front, slip these sts back to left-hand needle, purl these 3 sts.

▨	No stitch
■	Knit these sts when working first insert at beginning of row; omit these sts when working remaining repeats.
▨	Knit these sts when working last insert at end of row; omit these sts when working remaining repeats.
▨	Work from Insert Pattern Chart.
┃	Side edging vertical repeat
▌	Main pattern horizontal repeat
▌	Top edging horizontal repeat

INSERT PATTERN

center st

milanese shower bolero

SHAPING NOTE

When working shaping for the armholes, neck, and Sleeve caps, make sure to keep the Wing Stitch correct. In other words, if you cannot work a full decrease within the Wing Stitch (after working the shaping decreases), do not work the yo associated with that decrease in the pattern, and vice versa; work the sts in St st instead.

BACK

CO 52 (64, 76) sts. Knit 1 row. Purl 1 row. Knit 1 row.

(RS) K2, work Shower Stitch from Chart to last 2 sts, beginning with st 1 (7, 1) and ending with st 12 (6, 12) of Chart, k2. Work even, keeping first and last 2 sts of every row in St st, until 4 vertical repeats of Chart have been completed, ending with a WS row (piece should measure approximately 8 1/2" from the beginning). Knit 2 rows. Purl 1 row. Knit 1 row.

Shape Armholes (RS): K2 (4, 2), work Wing Stitch from Chart to last 2 (4, 2) sts, knit to end. Work even for 1 row.

SIZES LARGE/X-LARGE AND 2X/3X-LARGE ONLY (RS): Continuing in pattern as established, BO (2, 4) sts at beginning of next 2 rows—(60, 68) sts remain.

ALL SIZES (RS): Continuing in pattern as established, decrease 1 st each side this row, every other row 1 (3, 5) time(s), then every 4 rows 4 (3, 2) times, as follows: Ssk, work to last 2 sts, k2tog (see Shaping Note)—40 (46, 52) sts remain. Work even until armholes measure 7 (7 1/2, 8)", ending with a WS row.

Shape Shoulders and Neck (RS): BO 4 (6, 7) sts at beginning of next 2 rows, then 4 (5, 7) sts at beginning of next 2 rows. BO remaining 24 sts for Back neck.

LEFT FRONT

CO 28 (34, 40) sts. Knit 1 row. Purl 1 row. Knit 1 row.

(RS) K2, work Shower Stitch from Chart to last 2 sts, beginning with st 1 (7, 1) and ending with st 12 of Chart, k2. Work even for 11 rows, keeping first and last 2 sts of every row in St st.

(RS) Continuing in pattern as established, decrease 1 st at neck edge this row, then every 8 rows once, as follows: Work to last 2 sts, k2tog—26 (32, 38) sts remain. Work even until 4 vertical repeats of Chart have been completed, ending with a WS row (piece should measure approximately 8 1/2" from the beginning). Knit 2 rows. Purl 1 row. Knit 1 row.

Shape Armhole and Neck (RS): *Note: Armhole and neck shaping will be worked at the same time; please read entire section through before beginning.* K1 (4, 3), work Wing Stitch from Chart to last 1 (4, 3) st(s), knit to end. Work even for 1 row.

SIZES LARGE/X-LARGE AND 2X/3X-LARGE ONLY (RS): Continuing in pattern as established, BO (2, 4) sts, work to end—(30, 34) sts remain. Work even for 1 row.

ALL SIZES (RS): Continuing in pattern as established, decrease 1 st at armhole edge this row, every other row 1 (3, 5) time(s), then every 4 rows 4 (3, 2) times, as follows: Ssk, work to end. AT THE SAME TIME, decrease 1 st at neck edge this row, then every 3 rows 9 times, as follows: On RS rows, work to last 2 sts, k2tog; on WS rows, work to last 2 sts, p2tog—10 (13, 16) sts remain when all shaping is complete. Work even until armhole measures 7 (7 1/2, 8)", ending with a WS row.

Shape Shoulder (RS): BO 5 (7, 8) sts at armhole edge once, then 5 (6, 8) sts once.

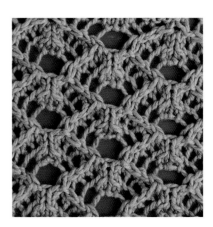

In Shower stitch, working "yo, k1, p1, yo" into a double yo of the previous row creates a large rounded eyelet. The pattern is stacked in a half-drop arrangement.

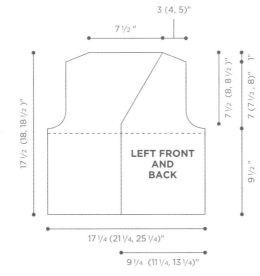

3 (4, 5)"

7 1/2 "

7 1/2 (8, 8 1/2)"

1"

7 (7 1/2, 8)"

17 1/2 (18, 18 1/2)"

LEFT FRONT AND BACK

9 1/2 "

17 1/4 (21 1/4, 25 1/4)"

9 1/4 (11 1/4, 13 1/4)"

12 1/2 (14 3/4, 17 3/4)"

5 1/4 (6 1/4, 7)"

18 1/4 (19, 19 3/4)"

SLEEVE

13 1/4"

11 1/2 "

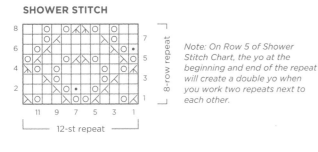

SHOWER STITCH

Note: On Row 5 of Shower Stitch Chart, the yo at the beginning and end of the repeat will create a double yo when you work two repeats next to each other.

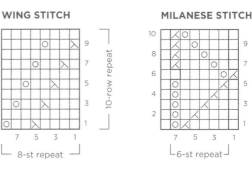

WING STITCH

MILANESE STITCH

BEAR TRACK PATTERN

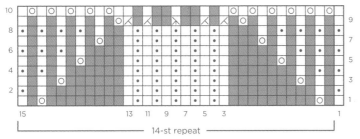

KEY

☐ Knit on RS, purl on WS.	⟋ Ssk on RS, p2tog-tbl on WS.
• Purl on RS, knit on WS.	⟍ Sk2p
⊙ Yo	▨ No stitch
⟍ K2tog on RS, p2tog on WS.	

RIGHT FRONT

CO 28 (34, 40) sts. Knit 1 row. Purl 1 row. Knit 1 row.

(RS) K2, work Shower Stitch from Chart to last 2 sts, beginning with st 1 and ending with st 12 (6, 12) of Chart, k2. Work even for 11 rows, keeping first and last 2 sts of every row in St st.

(RS) Continuing in pattern as established, decrease 1 st at neck edge this row, then every 8 rows once, as follows: Ssk, work to end—26 (32, 38) sts remain. Work even until 4 vertical repeats of Chart have been completed. Knit 2 rows. Purl 1 row. Knit 1 row.

Shape Armhole and Neck (RS): *Note: Armhole and neck shaping will be worked at the same time; please read entire section through before beginning.* K1 (4, 3), work Wing Stitch from Chart to last 1 (4, 3) st(s), knit to end.

SIZES LARGE/X-LARGE AND 2X/ 3X-LARGE ONLY (WS): Continuing in pattern as established, BO (2, 4) sts, work to end—(30, 34) sts remain.

ALL SIZES (RS): Continuing in pattern as established, decrease 1 st at armhole edge this row, every other row 1 (3, 5) time(s), then every 4 rows 4 (3, 2) times, as follows: Work to last 2 sts, k2tog. AT THE SAME TIME, decrease 1 st at neck edge this row, then every 3 rows 9 times, as follows:

Ssk, work to end—10 (13, 16) sts remain when all shaping is complete. Work even until armhole measures 7 (7 1/2, 8)", ending with a RS row.

Shape Shoulder (WS): BO 5 (7, 8) sts at armhole edge once, then 5 (6, 8) sts once.

SLEEVES

CO 40 sts. Knit 1 row. Purl 1 row. Knit 1 row.

(RS) K1 (edge st, keep in St st), work Milanese Stitch from Chart to last st, k1 (edge st, keep in St st). Work even until piece measures 4 (4, 3)" from the beginning, ending with a WS row.

Shape Sleeve (RS): Increase 1 st each side this row, then every 8 (4, 4) rows 1 (5, 10) time(s), as follows: K1, M1, work to last st, M1, k1—44 (52, 62) sts. Work even, working increased sts in St st as they become available, until piece measures 12" from the beginning, ending with a RS row. Knit 1 row. Purl 1 row. Knit 1 row.

Shape Cap

(RS) K2 (2, 3), work Wing Stitch from Chart to last 2 (2, 3) sts, knit to end. Work even for 1 row.

SIZES LARGE/X-LARGE AND 2X/ 3X-LARGE ONLY (RS): BO (2, 4) sts at beginning of next 2 rows—(48, 54) sts remain. Work even for 1 row.

ALL SIZES (RS): Continuing in pattern as established, decrease 1 st each side this row, every other row 7 (5, 4) times, then every row 8 (14, 20) times, as follows: On RS rows, ssk, work to last 2 sts, k2tog; on WS rows, p2tog, work to last 2 sts, p2tog-tbl. BO remaining 12 sts.

FINISHING

Block as desired. Sew shoulder seams.

Collar: With RS facing, using circ needle and beginning at bottom armhole edge of Right Front, pick up and knit 31 (37, 43) sts along CO edge of Right Front, 48 sts along Right Front neck edge, 24 sts along Back neck, 48 sts along Left Front neck edge, then 30 (36, 42) sts along CO edge of Left Front—181 (193, 205) sts. Cut yarn; do not turn. Slide sts to opposite end of needle. With RS facing, rejoin yarn. Begin Bear Track Pattern from Chart; work even until entire Chart is complete—406 (433, 460) sts. BO all sts, knitting all yos as you BO.

Sew side seams, sewing 1 1/2" of each end of Collar into side seam as you sew seam. *Note: Be sure to match CO edges of Fronts and Back when sewing side seams. Collar will make Fronts longer than Back once it is sewn into side seams.* Sew in Sleeves. Sew Sleeve seams.

tiger and snail folkloric blouse

ABBREVIATIONS

C4B: Slip 2 sts to cn, hold to back, k2, k2 from cn.

C4F: Slip 2 sts to cn, hold to front, k2, k2 from cn.

HIP BAND

Using larger needle, CO 19 sts. Begin Snail Shell Edging from Chart; work even until piece measures approximately 30 1/4 (33, 35 3/4, 38 1/2, 41 1/4)" from the beginning measured along straight edge, ending with Row 14 of Chart. BO all sts. Sew CO and BO edges together. Fold Band and lay flat, so that seam is at center back and snail shell motif is centered at center front, with scalloped edge nearest you and straight edge farthest away. Place marker at each fold, along straight edge, and at center of front snail shell motif. Left side marker will be on right side as the piece is lying flat; right side marker will be on left side.

BODY

With RS of front of Hip Band facing, using larger needle and beginning at left side marker, pick up and knit 32 (36, 40, 44, 48) sts to marker at center of snail shell motif, 1 st in center,

SIZES
Small (Medium, Large, X-Large, 2X-Large)

FINISHED MEASUREMENTS
38 (42, 46, 50, 54) bust
30 1/4 (33, 35 3/4, 38 1/2, 41 1/4)" high hip

Note: Blouse is intended to have 2-4" of ease in the bust. Choose the size to work based on your hip measurement.

YARN
Loop-d-Loop by Teva Durham Moss (85% extrafine merino wool / 15% nylon; 163 yards / 50 grams): 6 (7, 7, 8, 9) balls #10 Crimson

NEEDLES
One 29" (70 cm) long circular (circ) needle size US 10 (6 mm)
One 29" (70 cm) long circular needle size US 7 (4.5 mm)
Change needle size if necessary to obtain correct gauge.

NOTIONS
Stitch markers; cable needle (cn)

GAUGE
16 sts and 22 rows = 4" (10 cm) in Stockinette stitch (St st), using larger needles, after steam blocking

25 sts (before yos on Row 1) = 7 1/4" (18.5 cm) and 16 rows = 2 3/4" (7 cm) in Tiger Eye Pattern from Chart, using larger needles, after steam blocking

25 sts = 5 1/2" (14 cm) and 14 rows = 2 3/4" (7 cm) in Snail Shell Edging from Chart, using larger needles, after steam blocking

29 sts = 6 1/4" (16 cm) and 8 rows = 1 1/2" (4 cm) in Germaine Stitch from Chart, using larger needles, after steam blocking

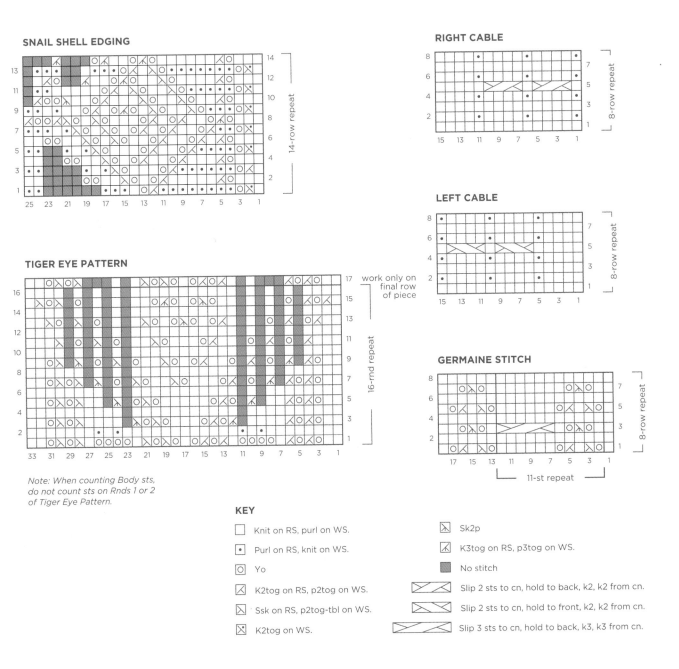

SNAIL SHELL EDGING

14-row repeat

TIGER EYE PATTERN

work only on final row of piece

16-rnd repeat

Note: When counting Body sts, do not count sts on Rnds 1 or 2 of Tiger Eye Pattern.

RIGHT CABLE

8-row repeat

LEFT CABLE

8-row repeat

GERMAINE STITCH

8-row repeat

11-st repeat

KEY

☐	Knit on RS, purl on WS.	⋋	Sk2p
•	Purl on RS, knit on WS.	⋌	K3tog on RS, p3tog on WS.
O	Yo	▨	No stitch
⋌	K2tog on RS, p2tog on WS.		Slip 2 sts to cn, hold to back, k2, k2 from cn.
⋋	Ssk on RS, p2tog-tbl on WS.		Slip 2 sts to cn, hold to front, k2, k2 from cn.
⋉	K2tog on WS.		Slip 3 sts to cn, hold to back, k3, k3 from cn.

32 (36, 40, 44, 48) sts to side marker, then 65 (73, 81, 89, 97) sts to next side marker—130 (146, 162, 178, 194) sts. Join for working in the rnd; place marker (pm) for beginning of rnd. Knit 1 rnd.

Next Rnd: K5 (9, 13, 17, 21), work 15 sts over Right Cable from Chart, work 25 sts over Tiger Eye Pattern from Chart, beginning with rnd 11 of Chart, work 15 sts over Left Cable from Chart, k5 (9, 13, 17, 21), slip marker (sm), knit to end. Work even for 9 rnds. *Note: Back is worked entirely in St st.*

Shape Bust

Increase Rnd: Increase 4 sts this rnd, then every 6 rnds 3 times, as follows: [K1-f/b, work to 1 st before marker, k1-f/b] twice—146 (162, 178, 194, 210) sts. *Note: When counting sts, do not count sts on Rnds 1 or 2 of Tiger Eye Pattern.* Work even, working increased sts in St st, until piece measures 14 1/2 (13 1/2, 12 3/4, 12, 11 1/4)" from the beginning, including Hip Band.

FRONT

Divide Front and Back: Work to marker, place next 73 (81, 89, 97, 105) sts on holder for Back—73 (81, 89, 97, 105) sts remain. Working on Front sts only, work even for 1 row.

Shape Armholes (RS): Continuing in patterns as established, decrease 1 st each side this row, every other row 5 (6, 8, 10, 12) times, then every 4 rows 7 (8, 8, 8, 8) times, as follows: Ssk, work to last 2 sts, k2tog—47 (51, 55, 59, 63) sts remain. Work even through Row 17 of Tiger Eye Pattern [armhole should measure approximately 7 1/2 (8 1/2, 9 1/4, 10, 10 3/4)"]. BO all sts.

12 ¾ (13 ½, 14 ½, 15 ½, 16 ½)"

7 ½ (8 ½, 9 ¼, 10, 10 ¾)"

FRONT AND BACK

9 (8, 7 ¼, 6 ½, 5 ¾)"

22"

HIP BAND

5 ½"

38 (42, 46, 50, 54)"

34 (38, 42, 46, 50)"

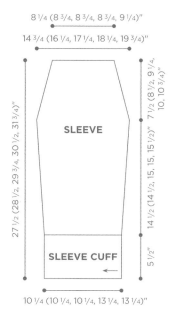

8 ¼ (8 ¾, 8 ¾, 8 ¾, 9 ¼)"

14 ¾ (16 ¼, 17 ¼, 18 ¼, 19 ¾)"

7 ½ (8 ½, 9 ¼, 10, 10 ¾)"

SLEEVE

27 ½ (28 ½, 29 ¾, 30 ½, 31 ¾)"

14 ½ (14 ½, 15, 15, 15 ½)"

SLEEVE CUFF

5 ½"

10 ¼ (10 ¼, 10 ¼, 13 ¼, 13 ¼)"

BACK

With RS of Back facing, rejoin yarn to sts on holder; work even for 2 rows. Shape armholes as for Front. Work even until piece measures same as for Front. BO all sts.

SLEEVE CUFF

Using larger needle, CO 19 sts. Begin Snail Shell Edging from Chart; work even until piece measures approximately 11 (11, 11, 13 ¾, 13 ¾)" from the beginning, ending with Row 14 of Chart. BO all sts.

SLEEVE

With RS of Sleeve Cuff facing, using larger needle and beginning at CO edge, pick up and knit 45 (45, 45, 57, 57) sts along straight side edge of Sleeve Cuff, ending at BO edge. Purl 1 row.

Row 1 (RS): K8 (8, 8, 14, 14), work Germaine Stitch from Chart to last 8 (8, 8, 14, 14) sts, knit to end.

Row 2: P8 (8, 8, 14, 14), work to last 8 (8, 8, 14, 14) sts, purl to end. Work even for 4 rows.

Shape Sleeve (RS): Increase 1 st each side this row, then every 6 (6, 4, 6, 6) rows 8 (11, 13, 9, 12) times, as follows: K1, M1, work to last st, M1, k1—63 (69, 73, 77, 83) sts. Work even until piece measures 20 (20, 20 ½, 20 ½, 21)" from the beginning, including Sleeve Cuff, ending with a WS row. Shape raglan Sleeve as for Front armholes. BO remaining 37 (39, 39, 39, 41) sts.

FINISHING

Block pieces lightly with steam, being careful not to flatten sts. Sew raglan seams. Sew sleeve seams.

Neckband: With RS facing, using smaller needle, and beginning at center Front neck edge, pick up and knit 22 (23, 24, 25, 26) sts along right Front neck edge, 28 (30, 32, 34, 36) sts along right Sleeve, 42 (44, 46, 48, 50) sts along Back neck edge, 28 (30, 32, 34, 36) sts along left Sleeve, and 22 (23, 24, 25, 26) sts along left Front neck edge—142 (150, 158, 166, 174) sts. Do not join. Purl 1 row.

Row 1 (RS): K1, *C4B; repeat from * to last st, k1.

Row 2: Purl.

Row 3: K3, *C4F; repeat from * to last 3 sts, k3.

Row 4: Purl.

Continuing in St st, work even until Neckband measures 2" from pick-up row, ending with a WS row. BO all sts.

Twisted Cord: Cut one strand of yarn 7 ½ (7 ½, 8, 8 ½, 8 ½) yards long. Fold strand in half and secure one end to stationary object. Twist from other end until it begins to buckle.

Three different types of faggoting are displayed here: There is openwork stranding of twisted rungs (every other row) at the top of the photo, single strand rungs (every row) in the edging at the bottom of the photo, as well as lovely interlinked strands across the straight edge of the edging.

Fold twisted length in half and holding ends together, allow to twist up on itself. Tie both ends in an overhand knot to secure; trim knotted ends.

Fold Neckband to WS, with Twisted Cord inserted under Neckband and loose ends of Cord at center Front. Sew Neckband to pick-up row, beginning at center Front.

shetland twins capelet

NOTE

The Shetland Twins chart (see Chart A, page 90) has lace patterning on both RS and WS rows.

STITCH PATTERN

2x2 Rib

(multiple of 4 sts + 2; 2-row repeat)

Row 1 (WS): Slip 1, p1, *k2, p2; repeat from * to end.

Row 2: Slip 1, k1, *p2, k2; repeat from * to end.

Repeat Rows 1 and 2 for 2x2 Rib.

BACK

CO 82 (90, 98, 106, 114) sts. Begin 2x2 Rib; work even until piece measures 3" from the beginning, ending with a WS row, decrease 1 st (p2tog) at center of last row—81 (89, 97, 105, 113) sts remain.

(RS) Work 8 sts in 2x2 Rib, knit to last 8 sts, work in 2x2 Rib to end. Work even as established, working first and last 8 sts in 2x2 Rib, and remaining sts in St st, until piece measures 12" from the beginning, ending with a WS row.

Shape Shoulders (RS): Continuing in pattern as established, decrease 1 st each side this row, every 4 rows 7 times, then every other row 0 (1, 2, 3, 4) times, as follows: Work 9 sts, ssk, work to last 11 sts, k2tog, work to end—65 (71, 77, 83, 89) sts remain. Work even until piece measures 18 (18 1/2, 19, 19 1/2, 20)" from the beginning, ending with a WS row.

Shape Saddles (RS): Work 10 sts, join a second ball of yarn, BO center 45 (51, 57, 63, 69) Back neck/shoulder sts, work to end—10 sts remain each side for saddle. Work even until saddles measure 3 (3 1/2, 4, 4 1/2, 5)". BO all sts.

FRONT

Work as for Back to end of bottom ribbing, ending with a WS row—81 (89, 98, 105, 113) sts remain.

(RS) Work 8 sts in 2x2 Rib, work in St st to last 8 sts, work in 2x2 Rib to end. Work even for 1 row.

SIZES

X-Small (Small, Medium, Large, X-Large)

FINISHED MEASUREMENTS

34 1/2 (38, 41, 44 1/2, 47 1/2)" around shoulders

MATERIALS

Tahki Yarns Donegal Tweed (100% pure new wool; 100 grams / 183 yards): 4 (4, 4, 5, 5) hanks #894 Dark Grey-Green

NEEDLES

One 29" (70 cm) long or longer circular (circ) needle size US 8 (5 mm)

Change needle size if necessary to obtain correct gauge.

NOTIONS

Stitch markers

GAUGE

15 sts and 22 rows = 4" (10 cm) in Stockinette stitch (St st)

Establish Lace Pattern, Shape Shoulders, and Shape Neck (RS): *Note: Lace Pattern and shoulder shaping are worked at the same time, then shoulder shaping and neck shaping are worked at the same time; please read entire section through before beginning.* Work 8 sts, k12 (16, 20, 24, 28), pm, referring to Chart A on page 90, work across sts 1–28 of Chart once, then sts 1–13 once, pm, knit to last 8 sts, work to end. Working Rib pattern, St st, and Chart pattern as established, work Rows 2–36 of Chart, then Rows 1–17.

(WS) Work 8 sts, work in St st to last 8 sts, removing markers, work to end. Work even for 2 rows. AT THE SAME TIME, when piece measures 12″ from the beginning, shape shoulders as for Back. AT THE SAME TIME, when piece measures 14″ from the beginning, ending with a WS row, begin neck shaping as follows.

Shape Neck (RS): Place marker either side of center 15 sts. Continuing with shoulder shaping, work to marker, join a second ball of yarn, BO center 15 sts, work to end. Working both sides at the same time and continuing with neck shaping, decrease 1 st each neck edge every 4 rows 3 times, then every other row 0 (1, 2, 3, 4) time(s), as follows: On left neck edge, work to last 3 sts, k2tog, k1; on right neck edge, k1, ssk, work to end—22 (24, 26, 28, 30) sts remain each side when shoulder and neck shaping are complete. Work even until piece measures 18 (18 ½, 19, 19 ½, 20)″ from the beginning, ending with a WS row.

Shape Saddles (RS): BO 12 (14, 16, 18, 20) sts each neck edge once—10 sts remain each side for saddle. Work even until saddles measure 3 (3 ½, 4, 4 ½, 5)″. BO all sts.

FINISHING
Block as desired.

Sew side seams, beginning 6″ up from bottom edge, leaving 6″ open for bottom slit. Sew side edges of saddles to BO edges of Front and Back.

COLLAR
With RS facing, beginning at bottom of right Front neck edge, pick up and knit 20 (22, 24, 26, 28) sts to saddle, 18 sts across both saddles, 22 (22, 26, 30, 30) sts across Back neck, 18 sts across both saddles, then 20 (22, 24, 26, 28) sts down left Front neck edge—98 (102, 110, 118, 122) sts.

Row 1 (WS): K0 (2, 0, 2, 0), *p2, k2; repeat from * to last 2 (4, 2, 4, 2) sts, p2, k0 (2, 0, 2, 0).

Row 2: Knit the knit sts and purl the purl sts as they face you. Work even until piece measures 3″ from pick-up row, ending with a WS row.

Shape Collar: *Note: Collar is shaped using short rows (see Special Techniques, page 154).*

Rows 1 (RS) and 2: Work to last 12 sts, wrp-t.

Rows 3–10: Work to 4 sts before wrapped st from row before last row worked, wrp-t.

Work across all sts, working wraps together with wrapped sts as you come to them on first row. Work even until piece measures 4″ from pick-up row, measured along side edge. BO all sts in pattern. Sew right-hand edge of Collar to BO sts at center Front; sew left-hand edge of Collar behind right.

Since this is an every-row lace pattern, the openwork around each hexagonal medallion has single-strand rungs, while the lace inside the medallions varies. Compare this swatch with the one on page 89 to see how it looks at a laceweight gauge. The outlines of the hexagons, formed by aligned decreases, are more pronounced at this heavier gauge.

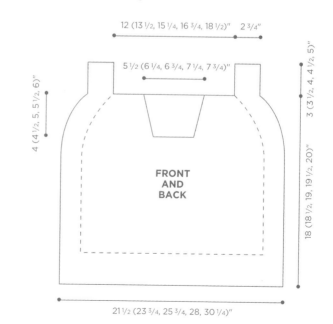

12 (13 ½, 15 ¼, 16 ¾, 18 ½)″ 2 ¾″

5 ½ (6 ¼, 6 ¾, 7 ¼, 7 ¾)″

4 (4 ½, 5, 5 ½, 6)″

3 (3 ½, 4, 4 ½, 5)″

18 (18 ½, 19, 19 ½, 20)″

FRONT AND BACK

21 ½ (23 ¾, 25 ¾, 28, 30 ¼)″

chevron and diamond jacket

NOTE
As you shape the Yoke, you will work several rows that will add stitches only to the Front and Back, then several rows that will add stitches only to the Sleeves, then you will end by adding stitches only to the Front and Back.

CARDIGAN
CO 2 sts for Left Front, pm, 5 sts for Left Sleeve, pm, 9 sts for Back, pm, 5 sts for Right Sleeve, pm, 2 sts for Right Front—23 sts. Purl 1 row.

Shape Yoke

Row 1 (RS): K1, yrn, knit to Sleeve marker, yo, sm, knit to Back marker, sm, yrn, knit to Sleeve marker, yo, sm, knit to Front marker, sm, yrn, knit to last st, yo, k1—29 sts (4 sts each Front, 5 sts each Sleeve, 11 sts for Back).

Note: When purling on WS rows, purl all yo increases through the back loop and all yrn increases through the front loop; this will twist the sts and close the holes. Purl all yos in the Charts through the front loop to keep the holes open.

Row 2: Purl.

Row 3: Slip 1, yrn, knit to Sleeve marker, yo, sm, knit to Back marker, sm, yrn, work Trellis Diamond Chart, beginning with st 2, and ending with st 14, yo, sm, knit to Front marker, sm, yrn, knit to last st, yo, k1—35 sts.

Row 4: Purl to end, CO 8 sts for Left Front—43 sts.

Row 5: Slip 1, knit to Sleeve marker, yo, sm, knit to Back marker, sm, yrn, pm for Chart, work across all 15 sts of Trellis Diamond Chart, pm for Chart, yo, sm, knit to Front marker, sm, yrn, k6, CO 13 sts for Right Front—60 sts (15 sts for Left Front, 5 sts each Sleeve, 15 sts for Back, 20 sts for Right Front).

Row 6 and all WS Rows: Repeat Row 2.

Row 7: Slip 1, knit to Sleeve marker, yo, sm, knit to Back marker, sm, yrn, work to Sleeve marker, yo, sm, knit to Front marker, sm, yrn, k3, pm for Chevron Feather Chart, work across all 21 sts of Chart (you will have only 17 sts but will increase 4 sts on first Chart row)—68 sts (16 sts for Left Front, 5 sts each Sleeve, 17 sts for Back, 25 sts for Right Front).

Rows 9, 11, 13, and 15: Slip 1, knit to Sleeve marker, sm, yrn, knit to Back marker, yo, sm, work to Sleeve marker, sm, yrn, knit to Front marker, yo, sm, work to end—84 sts after Row 15 (16 sts for Left Front, 13 sts each Sleeve, 17 sts for Back, 25 sts for Right Front).

Rows 17 and 19: Slip 1, knit to Sleeve marker, yo, sm, knit to Back marker, sm, yrn, work to Sleeve marker, yo, sm, knit to Front marker, sm, yrn, work to end—92 sts after Row 19 (18 sts for Left Front, 13 sts each Sleeve, 21 sts for Back, 27 sts for Right Front).

Row 20: Repeat Row 2.

The point of each chevron is formed by sk2p, a double decrease that emphasizes the angled lines at each side (rather than the center stitch). The remaining stitch, on close observation, extends from the stitch on the right edge of the previous row.

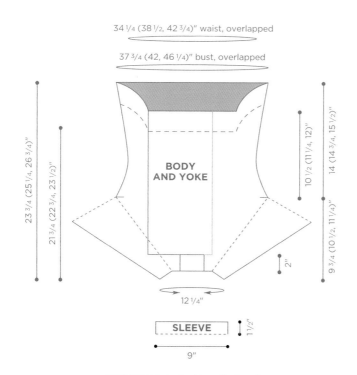

34 1/4 (38 1/2, 42 3/4)" waist, overlapped

37 3/4 (42, 46 1/4)" bust, overlapped

BODY AND YOKE

23 3/4 (25 1/4, 26 3/4)"

21 3/4 (22 3/4, 23 1/2)"

10 1/2 (11 1/4, 12)"

14 (14 3/4, 15 1/2)"

9 3/4 (10 1/2, 11 1/4)"

2"

12 1/4"

SLEEVE

1 1/2"

9"

Note: Piece is worked from the top down.

CHEVRON FEATHER

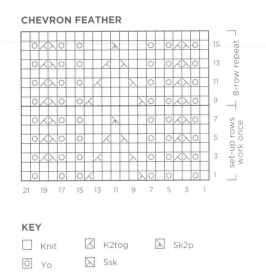

TRELLIS DIAMOND

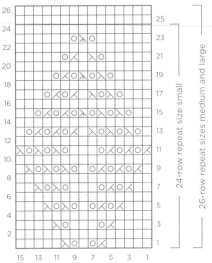

KEY

☐ Knit	⊠ K2tog	⋉ Sk2p
⊡ Yo	⊠ Ssk	

SIZES MEDIUM AND LARGE ONLY:
Repeat Rows 19 and 20 (once, twice)—(96, 100) sts [(19, 20) sts for Left Front, 13 sts each Sleeve, (23, 25) sts for Back, (28, 29) sts for Right Front].

ALL SIZES:
Divide Body and Sleeves (RS): Slip 1, knit to Sleeve marker, place Sleeve sts on holder, removing markers, CO 2 (3, 4) sts for underarm, pm for side, CO 2 (3, 4) sts, work to Sleeve marker, place Sleeve sts on holder, removing markers, CO 2 (3, 4) sts for underarm, pm for side, CO 2 (3, 4) sts, work to end—74 (82, 90) sts remain. Work even for 5 rows, slipping first st of every RS row, working sts from Charts as established, and working remaining sts in St st.

Shape Sides (RS): Decrease 4 sts this row, then every 4 rows twice, as follows: Slip 1, [work to 2 sts before side marker, ssk, sm, k2tog] twice, work to end—62 (70, 78) sts remain. Work even through Row 15 (15, 17) of Trellis Diamond Chart.

Shape Cutaway: *Note: Cutaway is shaped using short rows (see Special Techniques, page 154).*

Rows 1 (WS) and 2: Work to last 7 sts, wrp-t, work to last 13 sts, wrp-t.

Rows 3-8: Work to 3 sts before wrapped st from row before previous row, wrp-t.

(WS) Work across all sts, working wraps together with wrapped sts as you come to them.

(RS) Slip 1, [k1, p1] 7 (8, 9) times, [(k1, p1) into next st] 3 times, [(k1, p1) into next st] 3 times, *k1, p1; repeat from * to last st, k1—68 (76, 84) sts. Work even for 5 rows, slipping first st of every row, and knitting the knit sts and purling the purl sts as they face you. BO all sts in pattern.

SLEEVES
Transfer Sleeve sts to circ needle. With RS facing, rejoin yarn at armhole, pick up and knit 1 st from last st CO for underarm, *p1, k1; repeat from * to last st, p1, pick up and knit 1 st from first st CO for underarm—15 sts. Do not join. *Note: Leave center 2 (4, 6) sts CO for Body underarm unworked.*

(WS) M1, *p1, k1; repeat from * to last st, p1, M1—17 sts. BO all sts in pattern.

FINISHING
Block as desired. Sew half of each snap to WS of Right Front, 1 1/4" in from Front edge, the first snap 2" from the neck edge, the last snap 1" up from bottom edge, and the remaining 4 evenly spaced between. Sew other half of each snap to RS of Left Front, so that piece fits comfortably when Fronts are overlapped.

shetland shawl dress

NOTE
The Dress is made up of 11 Panels, five of which form the skirt of the Dress, and six of which form the Bodice. Each Panel is either worked off the initial Center Panel, or off a Panel that is picked up from the Center Panel.

SHAPING NOTE
When working shaping for the Middle Bodice Panels, make sure to keep the Chart pattern correct. In other words, if you cannot work a full decrease within the pattern (after working the shaping decreases), do not work the yo(s) associated with that decrease in the pattern, and vice versa; work the sts in St st instead.

STITCH PATTERN
Diamond Web Edging
(multiple varies; 6-row repeat)

Row 1 (RS): Pick up (but do not knit) 1 st from edge of Panel, k2tog (picked-up st together with first st of Diamond Web Edging), k1, yo, k2tog, k4, yo, k1, yo, k6—17 sts.

Row 2: K6, yo, [k3, yo, k2tog] twice, k1—18 sts.

Row 3: Pick up 1 st from edge of Panel, k2tog, k1, yo, k2tog, k1, k2tog, yo, k5, yo, k6—19 sts.

Row 4: BO 4 sts, k1, yo, ssk, k3, k2tog, [yo, k2tog, k1] twice—14 sts remain.

Row 5: Pick up 1 st from edge of Panel, k2tog, k1, yo, k2tog, k2, yo, ssk, k1, k2tog, yo, k2, [k1, p1] in next st—15 sts.

Row 6: K5, yo, sk2p, yo, k4, yo, k2tog, k1.

Repeat Rows 1-6 for Diamond Web Edging.

CENTER PANEL

CO 83 (97, 111, 125, 139) sts. Begin St st; work even for 1".

Row 1 (RS): Work 7 sts in St st, work 69 (83, 97, 111, 125) sts from Chart A, ending with st 13 (27, 13, 27, 13) of Chart, work in St st to end.

Work even until 5 (6, 7, 8, 9) vertical repeats of Chart A have been completed. Change to St st across all sts; work even for 1". BO all sts.

WAIST PANEL

Fold Center Panel in half lengthwise, with CO and BO edges together; mark fold along both edges (this will mark right side of Dress). With RS facing, beginning at CO edge, pick up and knit 82 (98, 114, 130, 146) sts to marker, 1 st at marker (this will be center st indicated in Chart B), then 82 (98, 114, 130, 146) sts to BO edge—165 (197, 229, 261, 293) sts. Purl 1 row.

Begin pattern from Chart B; work through center st, working increases and decreases as indicated in Chart, then reverse Chart, beginning with st before center st, and working back to st 1, working ssk instead of k2tog and k2tog instead of ssk. Do not reverse sk2p. Work even until entire Chart is complete—183 (215, 247, 279, 311) sts.

BOTTOM PANEL

With RS of Center Panel facing, beginning at BO edge, pick up and knit 82 (98, 114, 130, 146) sts to marker, 1 st at marker (this will be center st indicated in Chart C), then 82 (98, 114, 130, 146) sts to BO edge—165 (197, 229, 261, 293) sts. Purl 1 row. Begin pattern from Chart C; work as for Waist Panel, reversing Chart after working through center st. Work even until entire Chart is complete—217 (249, 281, 313, 345) sts.

FRONT SIDE PANEL

With RS of Center Front Panel facing, pick up and knit 86 (102, 118, 134, 150) sts along CO edge of Center Front Panel. Purl 1 row.

Row 1 (RS): Work 3 sts in St st, work pattern from Chart B to end, beginning with st 35 and working in reverse to st 1.

Work even until entire Chart is complete—95 (111, 127, 143, 159) sts. BO all sts.

BACK SIDE PANEL

With RS of Center Front Panel facing, pick up and knit 86 (102, 118, 134, 150) sts along BO edge of Center Front Panel. Purl 1 row.

Row 1 (RS): Work pattern from Chart B to last 3 sts, beginning with st 1 and ending with st 35, work 3 sts in St st.

Work even until entire Chart is complete—95 (111, 127, 143, 159) sts. BO all sts.

Sew side edges of Front and Back Side Panels and Waist Panel.

LOWER BODICE PANEL

With RS of Waist Panel facing, beginning at Waist Panel seam, pick up and knit 95 (111, 127, 143, 159) sts to center st of Waist Panel, 1 st in center st, then 95 (111, 127, 143, 159) sts to seam—191 (223, 255, 287, 319) sts. Join for working in the rnd; place marker (pm) for beginning of rnd. Begin pattern from Chart D; work as for Waist Panel, reversing Chart after working through center st. Work even until entire Chart is complete—195 (227, 259, 291, 323) sts. Knit 1 rnd, decrease 0 (2, 4, 6, 8) sts evenly spaced to center st, then 0 (2, 4, 6, 8) sts evenly spaced to end—195 (223, 251, 279, 307) sts remain.

MIDDLE FRONT BODICE PANEL

Work pattern from Chart E through center st, place remaining 97 (111, 125, 139, 153) sts on holder for Middle Back Bodice Panel. Working back and forth, work even for 3 rows.

Shape Panel (RS): Decrease 1 st at beginning of row this row, then every other row 17 (15, 13, 13, 11) times, as follows: Ssk, work to end (see

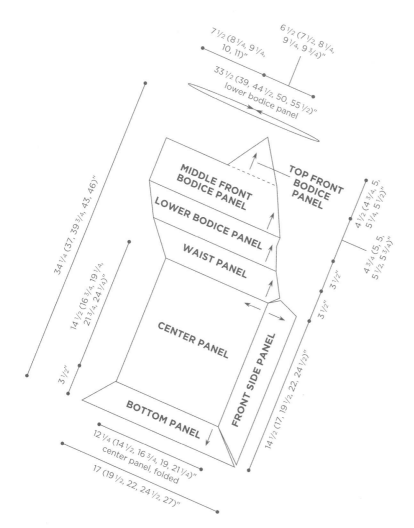

Shaping Note)—80 (96, 112, 126, 142) sts remain.

SIZES MEDIUM, LARGE, X-LARGE, AND 2X-LARGE ONLY (RS):
Decrease 2 sts at beginning of row this row, then every other row (2, 5, 7, 10) times, as follows: Sssk, work to end—(90, 100, 110, 120) sts remain.

ALL SIZES (WS): Work even for 2 rows. BO 41 (45, 51, 55, 61) sts, work to end—39 (45, 49, 55, 59) sts remain.

TOP FRONT BODICE PANEL
(RS) K9 (12, 14, 17, 19), pm, k21, pm, knit to end. Purl 1 row.

Shape Panel (RS): Ssk, knit to marker, work across Chart F to next marker, knit to last 2 sts, k2tog—37 (43, 47, 53, 57) sts remain. Work even for 1 row.

(RS) Decrease 1 st each side this row, then every other row 16 (15, 15, 16, 16) times, as follows: Ssk, work to last 2 sts, k2tog—3 (11, 15, 19, 23) sts remain. Work even for 1 row. Do not turn.

SIZES MEDIUM, LARGE, X-LARGE, AND 2X-LARGE ONLY (RS):
Decrease 2 sts each side this row, then every other row (1, 2, 3, 4) times, as follows: Sssk, work to last 3 sts, k3tog—3 sts remain. Work even for 1 row.

ALL SIZES (RS): Continue in I-Cord as follows until strap measures 10 (10 1/4, 10 1/2, 10 3/4, 11)": K3; do not turn. *Slide sts to opposite end of needle, knit sts from right to left, pulling yarn from left to right for first st. Do not turn; repeat from *. BO all sts, leaving a 20" tail to adjust length of I-Cord if necessary. With RS facing, beginning at first 3 BO sts of Middle Front Bodice Panel, pick up and knit 3 sts; work I-Cord as for first strap.

MIDDLE BACK BODICE PANEL
With RS facing, rejoin yarn to sts on holder, pick up and knit 1 st, work pattern from Chart E to end, beginning with st 2 of Chart. Work even for 3 rows.

Shape Panel (RS): Decrease 1 st at beginning of row this row, then every other row 17 (15, 13, 13, 11) times, as follows: Ssk, work to end—80 (96, 112, 126, 142) sts remain.

SIZES MEDIUM, LARGE, X-LARGE, AND 2X-LARGE ONLY (RS):
Decrease 2 sts at beginning of row this row, then every other row (2, 5, 7, 10) times, as follows: Sssk, work to end—(90, 100, 110, 120) sts remain.

ALL SIZES (WS): Work even for 3 rows. BO 41 (45, 51, 55, 61) sts, work to end—39 (45, 49, 55, 59) sts remain.

TOP BACK BODICE PANEL
Purl 1 row.

(RS) K9 (12, 14, 17, 19), pm, k21, pm, knit to end. Purl 1 row.

Shape Panel (RS): Ssk, knit to marker, work across Chart F to next marker, knit to last 2 sts, k2tog—37 (43, 47, 53, 57) sts remain. Work even for 1 row.

(RS) Decrease 1 st each side this row, then every other row 16 (15, 15, 16, 16) times, as follows: Ssk, work to last 2 sts, k2tog—3 (11, 15, 19, 23) sts remain. Work even for 1 row. Do not turn.

SIZES MEDIUM, LARGE, X-LARGE, AND 2X-LARGE ONLY (RS):
Decrease 2 sts each side this row, then every other row (1, 2, 3, 4) times, as follows: Sssk, work to last 3 sts, k3tog—3 sts remain. Work even for 1 row. BO all sts.

BOTTOM EDGING PANEL
CO 15 sts. With RS facing, beginning at seam between Back and Front Side Panels, work Diamond Web Edging along BO edge of Front Side Panel, Bottom Panel, then Back Side Panel, working 1 st of BO edge together with the first st of every RS row of Diamond Web Edging. *Note: Pick up approximately 1 st for every 2 BO sts along straight edges, and 1 st for every BO st around corners. Adjust number of BO sts to skip between pick-ups if necessary to ensure that edge lies flat.* BO all sts. Sew BO edge to CO edge.

Adjust length of straps if necessary. Sew BO edge of straps to Back Panels, in same position as on Front Panels. Block piece as desired.

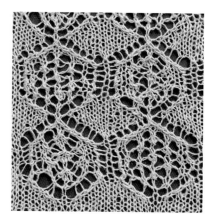

Rows of hexagonal medallions—alternately filled with sheer diamond mesh or solid stacked diamonds—create solid Stockinette stitch diamond cutouts between their tiers.

CHART A

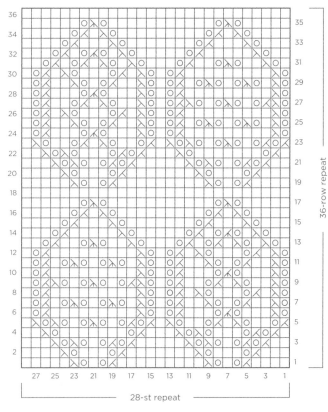

36-row repeat

28-st repeat

Note: Charts B, C, and D are written for half the number of sts worked over those Charts. In each case, you will work to the marked center st, then reverse the Chart, beginning with the st before the center st, and working back to st 1. When working in reverse, you will work ssk instead of k2tog and k2tog instead of ssk. You will not reverse sk2p.

KEY

☐	Knit on RS, purl on WS.
⊙	Yo
⩒	[K1, p1, k1] in next st.
⧄	K2tog on RS, p2tog on WS.
⧅	Ssk on RS, p2tog-tbl on WS.
⧄	K3tog on RS, p3tog on WS.
⋏	Sk2p

CHART B

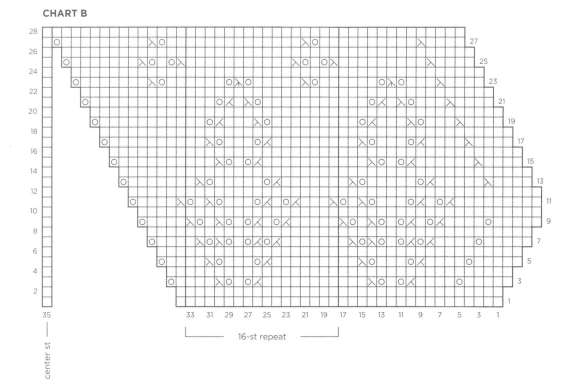

16-st repeat

center st

CHART C

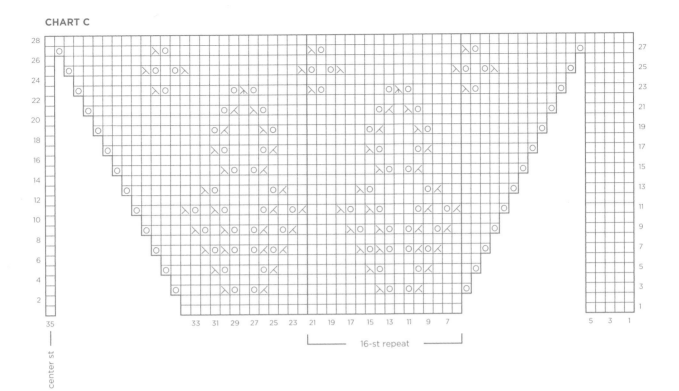

center st

16-st repeat

CHART D

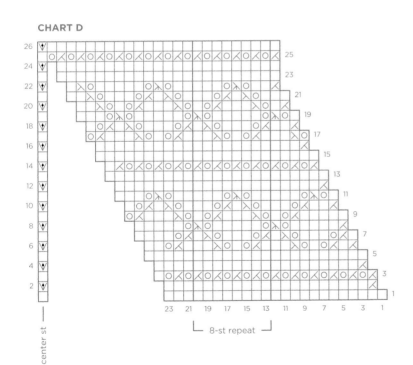

center st

8-st repeat

CHART E

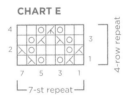

4-row repeat

7-st repeat

CHART F

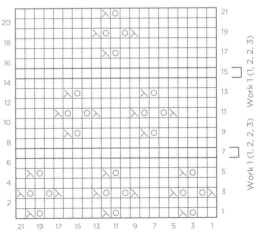

Work 1 (1, 2, 2, 3)   Work 1 (1, 2, 2, 3)

LEAVES

Botany in Stitches

THE LEAF HAS BEEN A SIGNIFICANT MOTIF FOR ARTISANS SINCE ANCIENT times, as evidenced by the acanthus foliage on Corinthian columns and ginkgo leaves on Japanese pottery. These botanical elements are treasured for their symbolism (representing valor, victory, peace, plenty, new life) as well as for their decorative surface design. Knitters have also found ways to immortalize the leaf. The fifteen-year anniversary issue of *Vogue Knitting* in 1997—which is coincidentally the issue in which my first design appeared—featured a story called "Autumn Splendor," in which I learned that leaves are a perennial knitwear theme. After looking at the story, I added leaves to my list of themes to explore one day. Little did I know that when I launched Loop-d-Loop just a few years later with my first accessory, the Lace Leaf Cravat (reproduced here on page 104), I would become known for my work with lace leaf patterns.

Over the years I have discovered a variety of leaf pattern possibilities and I am delighted to give them their own chapter here with easy, quick accessories as well as more complex sweaters in a variety of yarns, from fine-gauge cotton, to hand-dyed silk, to superbulky wool. I sifted through hundreds of leaf patterns in stitch dictionaries in search of several to present here. Many of the knitted leaves that I explored were variations of one another, presented as a pointed oval with increases creating the widening fullness and decreases creating the pointed tip. They also typically had eyelets running up their centers to represent the leaf's central vein, with branching veins extending to each side. But their range was still staggering—some big, some small; some paired along vertical or horizontal branches; some arranged at alternating intervals from side to side; some worked as a cluster; some aligned in garden plot rows. Many of these patterns used a background of purl stitches so that the knitted leaf appears embossed.

Some of the more interesting leaf patterns are not found in stitch dictionaries, but rather in the doilies of Marianne Kinzel and Herbert Niebling. There one can find elaborate scroll-like leaves with complex undulating edges as well as fernlike patterns with ladder stitch delineating each frond. For instance, I've done my own variation on the stylized Rose Leaf pattern used in a curtain by Kinzel for the Art Deco Leaves Cardigan on page 116.

lace leaf cravat

I first started my Loop-d-Loop line in 2000 with sculptural neckpieces such as cowls, capelets, and cravats. At the time, retailers such as Banana Republic were featuring the keyhole scarf—a short scarf where one tip is pulled through a slit in the other end—and knitting magazines followed suit. I liked that these small-scale keyhole scarves resembled men's cravats, and noted that the tapered ends often resembled the shape of a leaf. Knitting a leaf motif at each end of the scarf was the logical next step. This signature pattern of mine is a great beginning lace project and can now be worked following a chart instead of written-out instructions (as the original pattern appeared).

>> See pattern on page 104.

feather mitts

This feathery stitch pattern within a ground of openwork is sometimes called Trellis Framed Leaf. Whether you interpret it as a feather's quill or leaf's vein, the strong central ridge in the oblong oval is captivating, particularly where the ridge and the trellis framework morph into one another. To create this transition, the inventor of the stitch pattern had to shift cleverly from an even number to an odd number of stitches. These mitts are a good way to transform an odd skein of yarn from your stash into a gift or perhaps an indulgence for yourself. They can be worn two ways—with the lace toward the fingertips or toward the wrist.

>> See pattern on page 106 .

embossed leaves wrap

This wrap is my deconstruction of the well-known Garden Plot square. Typically used in bedspreads or blankets and done in fine white cotton or colorful wool, the Garden Plot square is a counterpane patchwork design consisting of directional, embossed leaves. Bedspreads and blankets done in this popular design abound at vintage stores, and in the movie *The Other Side of Midnight*, the ingénue, Noelle, snuggles under a Garden Plot blanket in a Paris atelier during World War II.

The Garden Plot in this version begins with a single leaf at one corner and continues with evenly spaced embossed leaves, landscaped with ridged stripes of eyelet that grow outward to form a triangle. The addition of an opposing triangle at the other edge make a dumbbell-shaped wrap that is a deconstruction of the traditional triangle-shaped shawl. In this instance, rather than a point at center back, there are inverted triangles at each end that can be worn to form a poncholike triangle at front. Alternatively, it can be worn wrapped around the neck or draped and belted to form an apronlike vest. The striated colors of hand-painted yarn accentuate the directional knitting.

>> See pattern on page 108.

split leaves ottoman cover

Like the tessellated images of M. C. Escher, this Split Leaf pattern is a visual puzzle. The geometric leaves form an intriguing tiled grid—the edge of one leaf becomes the center of the next, making it hard to tell which leaves are in the foreground. The purl-stitch center veins and the eyelet outlines form triangular shapes that, to me, resemble little Eiffel Towers. Simple square ottomans are easy to find at retail shops; this is a way to give yours a cozy look. Alternatively, you can work a straight panel of this magnified lace to create a wintry throw.

>> See pattern on page 110.

closed bud pullover

The Closed Bud pattern features a flower bud with a rounded base, but it is the bending leaves—a long lancelike pair that fold away from each other like those of a tulip—that come to the foreground. The feathering directional decreases and twisted stitches create a raised effect, reminding me of terra-cotta reliefs on Art Deco buildings. In Barbara Walker's *Second Treasury of Knitting Patterns,* the stitch pattern is credited to Dorothy Reade of Oregon. Reade was a pioneering lace knitter who developed charting techniques and advocated for charts. She was the subject of Donna Druchunas's book *Arctic Lace,* which delves into Reade's work in the 1960s to help the Alaskan natives build trade in musk ox fiber (qiviut) and knitted lace.

In a pattern arrangement influenced by Victorian high-neck blouses, I isolated a column of Closed Bud up the center front and along the sleeves. The pattern broadens into an allover design at the bust, then morphs into more delicate lace at the shoulders. I searched many small, denticulated patterns to find a match that would fit atop the main pattern and decided on this one: a stitch repeat that could be centered without too much adjustment in the transition row and also a small-scale pattern that could hold its own, competing for visual interest while enhancing the lines of the previous pattern band. A crisp, mercerized cotton yarn allows for great stitch detail.

>> See pattern on page 112.

art deco leaves cardigan

For this jacket, I began with a stitch pattern found on a curtain designed by Marianne Kinzel that featured rose leaves stylized into tilted rhomboids with an Art Deco feel. The Art Deco style was named for the 1925 Paris exposition of decorative arts. At that time, the new aviation and automobile industries were influencing all aspects of design—from architecture to clothing to home goods—with streamlined and metallic elements, aeronautical "speed lines" and other sculptural winglike repeating patterns. In this cardigan, the geometric feel of the branched leaves and slinky silver silk yarn go along with these themes. I adjusted the stitch patterns that filled the spaces in between leaves, interspersing Trellis Diamond with a Quatrefoil Diamond—to me, these pattern elements between the leaves have the feel of filigree jewelry settings. For a body-conscious fit, I worked the bodice up from the waist and then worked the jacket skirt down from the smaller waist repeat. This mirrored construction also resulted in large diamond-shaped medallions that draw the eye to the waist. The sleeve features the same construction, so after working the upper sleeve, you can choose a more formal or dramatic look by working either one or two repeats downward.

>> See pattern on page 116.

lace leaf cravat

FINISHED MEASUREMENTS
38" long

YARN
Cascade Yarns Cascade 220 (100% wool; 220 yards / 100 grams): 1 hank #2435 Japanese Maple

NEEDLES
One pair straight needles size US 13 (9 mm)
Change needle size if necessary to obtain correct gauge.

GAUGE
14 sts and 20 rows = 4" (10 cm) in Stockinette stitch (St st), using 2 strands of yarn held together

NOTE
You may work Leaf Pattern and Garter Pattern from text or Charts.

STITCH PATTERNS
Leaf Pattern (see Chart)
(st count varies; 27 rows)

Row 1 (WS): K2, p3, k2.

Row 2: Knit.

Row 3: K2, p3, k2.

Row 4: K2, yo, k3, yo, k2—9 sts.

Row 5 and all RS Rows through Row 23: K2, purl to last 2 sts, k2.

Row 6: K1, k2tog, yo, k3, yo, ssk, k1.

Row 8: [K2, yo] twice, k1, [yo, k2] twice—13 sts.

Row 10: K2, yo, k4, yo, k1, yo, k4, yo, k2—17 sts.

Row 12: K3, yo, ssk, k3, yo, k1, yo, k3, k2tog, yo, k3—19 sts.

Row 14: K4, yo, ssk, k7, k2tog, yo, k4.

Row 16: K2, k3tog-tbl, yo, ssk, k5, k2tog, yo, k3tog, k2—15 sts remain.

Row 18: K2, ssk, yo, ssk, k3, k2tog, yo, k2tog, k2—13 sts remain.

Row 20: K2, ssk, yo, ssk, k1, k2tog, yo, k2tog, k2—11 sts remain.

Row 22: K2, ssk, yo, s2kp2, yo, k2tog, k2—9 sts remain.

Row 24: K2, ssk, k1, k2tog, k2—7 sts remain.

Row 25: K2, p3tog, k2—5 sts remain.

Row 26: K1, p3tog, k1—3 sts remain.

Row 27: K3tog—1 st remains.

Garter Pattern (see Chart)
(panel of 9 sts; 18-row repeat)

Rows 1, 3, and 5 (WS): Knit.

Row 2 and all RS Rows: Knit.

Rows 7, 9, 11, 13, 15, and 17: K2, p5, k2.

Row 18: Knit.

Repeat Rows 1-18 for Garter Pattern.

FIRST LEAF

Using 2 strands of yarn held together, CO 7 sts. Begin Leaf Pattern from text or Chart; work even until Leaf is complete. Fasten off.

BODY

With RS facing, using 2 strands of yarn held together, pick up and knit 9 sts along CO edge of Leaf—9 sts. Begin Garter Pattern from text or Chart; work Rows 1-18 six times, then Rows 1-5 once.

Decrease Row (RS): K1, k2tog, k3, ssk, k1—7 sts remain.

SECOND LEAF

Change to Leaf Pattern from text or Chart; work even until Leaf is complete. Fasten off.

FINISHING

Block as desired.

A wide textural edge frames an inner leaf, reminiscent of a paisley. The inner leaf has a vein depicted by yarnovers, and a spadelike outline drawn with inward-pointing decreases.

LEAF PATTERN

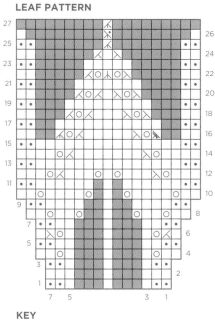

GARTER PATTERN

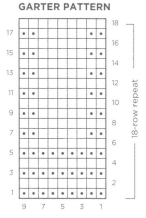

18-row repeat

KEY

☐	Knit on RS, purl on WS.	⟋	Ssk
•	Purl on RS, knit on WS.	⟋	K3tog on RS, p3tog on WS.
○	Yo	⟍	K3tog-tbl
▨	No stitch	⅄	S2kp2
⟋	K2tog	⟋	P3tog on RS.

feather mitts

HAND

Note: As shown, piece is worked from the wrist to the hand.

CO 41 sts. Begin St st, beginning with a purl row; work even for 3 rows.

Turning Row (WS): *K2tog, yo; repeat from * to last st, k1. Work even in St st for 3 rows, decrease 1 st on last row—40 sts remain.

Next Row (WS): *P2tog (1 st from CO row together with 1 st on needle); repeat from * to end.

Begin Chart

Next Row (RS): K1 (edge st, keep in St st), work Feather and Trellis Pattern from Chart across 38 sts, k1 (edge st, keep in St st). Work Rows 2-32 once, then Rows 1 and 2 once.

WRIST

Decrease Row (RS): K6, [ssk] twice, k1, [k2tog] twice, k10, [ssk] twice, k1, [k2tog] twice, knit to end—32 sts remain. Work even in St st for 3 rows.

Increase Row (RS): K1, M1, k6, [M1, k1] 4 times, k11, [M1, k1] 4 times, knit to last st, M1, k1—42 sts.

Work even in St st for 2". BO all sts.

FINISHING

Block pieces. Sew side edges.

SIZES

One size fits most

FINISHED MEASUREMENTS

7 ½" circumference at widest point

YARN

Lorna's Laces Green Line DK (100% organic merino wool; 145 yards / 2 ounces): 1 hank Mirth

NEEDLES

One pair straight needles size US 3 (3.25 mm)

Change needle size if necessary to obtain correct gauge.

GAUGE

20 sts and 28 rows = 4" (10 cm) over Feather and Trellis Pattern from Chart, slightly stretched

FEATHER AND TRELLIS PATTERN

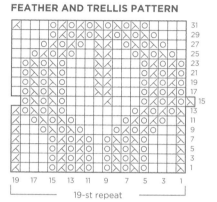

KEY

Note: Chart shows only RS rows. Purl all sts on WS rows.

☐ Knit

Ⓞ Yo

◩ K2tog

◪ Ssk

The solid fabric moves inward on a diagonal toward the central "quill," while the quill is delineated by "feathered" decreases that point outward.

embossed leaves wrap

NOTE

Each edge is worked as a triangle, then stitches are cast on for the center back, the two triangles are joined by the center back, and the piece is worked down to the bind-off edge, with shaping worked at five points. Instructions are included to make the Wrap longer if you wish. If you choose to do so, remember to purchase additional yarn.

EDGE TRIANGLE (make 2)
CO 3 sts. Knit 1 row.

Shape Triangle

(RS) Begin Embossed Leaves Pattern from Chart; work even through Row 38 of Chart—45 sts. *Note: To make Embossed Leaf motifs easier to work, you may want to place a marker on either side of Leaf.*

Place sts on st holder for first Triangle; leave sts on needle for second Triangle.

WRAP

Row 39 (RS): Continuing with Chart, work to end of second Triangle, pm for Back, CO 39 (59) sts for Back, pm for Back, work across first Triangle from st holder—121 (141) sts.

Rows 40-42: Work to first Back marker, knit to next Back marker, work to end.

Row 43 (RS): Work to first Back marker, sm, [yo, k2tog] 10 (15) times, pm for center Back, k1, [yo, k2tog] 9 (14) times, yo, sm, work to end—126 (146) sts.

Row 44: Work to first Back marker, knit to last Back marker, work to end.

Row 45: Work across Row 23 of Chart to first Back marker, sm, work to 1 st before center Back marker across sts outlined in blue on Row 23 of Main Chart, k1, sm, k1, work to last Back marker across sts outlined in blue, sm, work across Row 23 of Chart to end—134 (154) sts.

Rows 46-64: Work even until Row 42 of Chart is complete—206 (226) sts after Row 63.

SIZES
Small/Medium
(Large/X-Large)

FINISHED MEASUREMENTS
70 1/2 (75 1/2)" wide at bottom edge x 7" deep at back

YARN
Artyarns Silk Rhapsody Glitter (80% silk / 20% mohair; 260 yards / 100 grams): 2 (2) hanks #114

NEEDLES
One 29" (70 cm) long or longer circular (circ) needle size US 6 (4 mm)

Change needle size if necessary to obtain correct gauge.

NOTIONS
Stitch markers; stitch holder or spare circular needle

GAUGE
16 sts and 22 rows = 4" (10 cm) in Stockinette stitch (St st)

Row 65 (RS): Work Row 43 of Chart to first Back marker, sm, work to last Back marker across sts outlined in blue on Row 43, sm, work Row 43 to end.

Row 66: Work even.

Rows 67-88: Repeat Rows 45-66—286 (306) sts after Row 83. *Note: If you wish to work another tier of* embossed leaves, repeat Rows 45-66 *once more. If you add another tier, the Back will measure 10 ½" deep.*

Knit 2 rows. BO all sts knitwise.

FINISHING
Block lightly.

Individual leaves worked in Stockinette stitch on a background of Reverse Stockinette stitch pop up off the surface for an embossed effect.

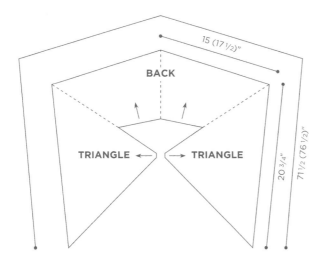

EMBOSSED LEAVES PATTERN

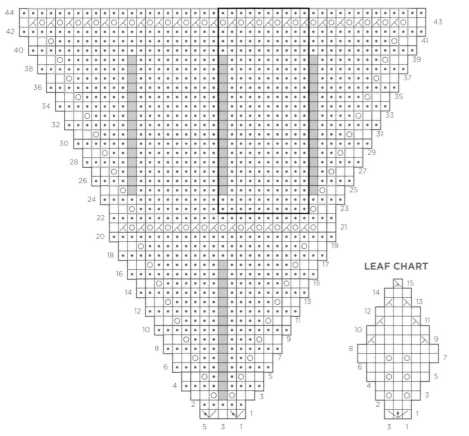

LEAF CHART

KEY

☐	Knit on RS, purl on WS.
•	Purl on RS, knit on WS.
O	Yo
⧄	K2tog
⧅	Ssk
⧄	Sk2p
⟱	[K1, p1] in next st.
⟱	[K1, p1, k1] in next st.
▧	Embossed Leaf – work from Leaf Chart.
|	Work across these sts for Back as indicated in text.
|	Stitch repeat

split leaves ottoman cover

TOP

CO 37 sts. Begin Split Leaf Pattern from Chart; work even until you have completed 3 vertical repeats of Chart (piece should measure approximately 21″ from the beginning).

SIDES

(RS) Continuing with Chart, work to end, CO 108 sts—145 sts. Working CO sts in pattern from Chart, work even until piece measures 16″ from CO for Sides, or to desired length. BO all sts.

FINISHING

Block lightly with steam. Place marker every 36 sts (every 3 pattern repeats) along CO edge of Sides. Pin CO edge at markers to corners of Top. Sew 3 open sides of Top to CO edge of Sides. Sew Side edges together.

SIZES

Designed to fit the IKEA Klippan Footstool and other common cube ottomans

FINISHED MEASUREMENTS

21″ square across top x 16″ high

YARN

Loop-d-Loop by Teva Durham Tundra (100% extrafine merino wool; 35 yards / 50 grams): 17 balls #01 Natural

NEEDLES

One pair straight needles size US 15 (10 mm)

Change needle size if necessary to obtain correct gauge.

GAUGE

12 sts and 16 rows = 7″ (18 cm) over Split Leaf Pattern from Chart, slightly stretched

SPLIT LEAF PATTERN

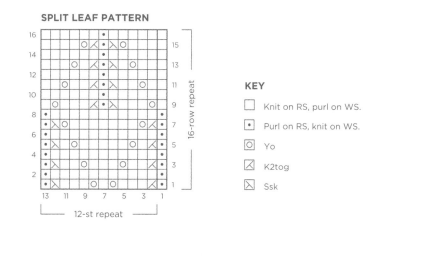

KEY

☐	Knit on RS, purl on WS.
▪	Purl on RS, knit on WS.
Ⓞ	Yo
⟋	K2tog
⟍	Ssk

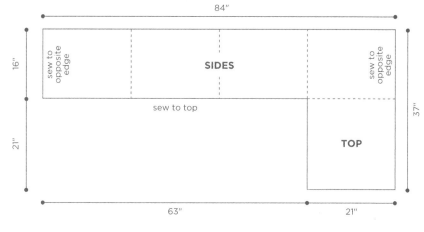

In this staggered, visual puzzle, each leaf is split by a purl stitch vein that becomes the outline of another leaf in the arrangement.

closed bud pullover

SIZES
Small (Medium/Large, X/2X-Large, 3X/4X-Large)

FINISHED MEASUREMENTS
35 1/2 (42 1/2, 49 1/2, 56 1/2)" bust

YARN
Filatura Di Crosa Millefili Fine (100% cotton; 137 yards / 50 grams): 10 (11, 13, 14) balls #155 Light Blue

NEEDLES
One pair straight needles size US 2 (2.75 mm)

One pair straight needles size US 3 (3.25 mm)

One pair straight needles size US 7 (4.5 mm)

Change needle size if necessary to obtain correct gauge.

NOTIONS
Crochet hook size US C/2 (2.75 mm); waste yarn; stitch markers; stitch holders; six 1/4" buttons

GAUGE
22 sts = 3 1/2" (9 cm) and 26 rows = 3" (7.5 cm) in Closed Bud Pattern from Chart, using size US 3 needles

25 sts and 35 rows = 4" (10 cm) in Stockinette stitch (St st), using size US 3 needles

SHAPING NOTE

When working shaping for the arm-holes, neck, and sleeve cap, make sure to keep the Closed Bud Pattern correct. In other words, if you cannot work a full decrease within the Closed Bud Pattern (after working the shaping decreases), do not work the yo(s) associated with that decrease in the pattern, and vice versa; work the sts in St st instead. Note that sometimes the increase and its associated decrease are separated from each other by several sts.

BACK

Using size US 2 needles and Provisional CO (see Special Techniques, page 154), CO 115 (137, 159, 181) sts.

Rows 1 and 3 (RS): Knit.

Rows 2 and 6: Purl.

Row 4 (Turning Row): Change to size US 7 needles. Purl.

Row 5: Change to size US 2 needles. Knit.

Row 7: Unravel Provisional CO. Fold hem to WS. *K2tog (1 st on needle together with 1 st from CO); repeat from * to end.

Row 8: Change to size US 3 needles. Purl.

Shape Waist (RS): Continuing in St st, decrease 1 st each side this row, then every 12 rows 3 times, as follows: K1, k2tog, knit to last 3 sts, ssk, k1—107 (129, 151, 173) sts remain. Work even for 1 row.

(RS) Increase 1 st each side this row, then every 12 rows once, as follows: K1, k1-f/b, knit to last 3 sts, k1-f/b, k2—111 (133, 155, 177) sts. Work even until 78 rows have been worked from beginning of waist shaping, ending with a WS row.

Begin Closed Bud Pattern (RS): Change to Closed Bud Pattern from Chart, beginning as indicated in Chart. Work Rows 1-26 once.

SIZES MEDIUM/LARGE, X/2X-LARGE, AND 3X/4X-LARGE ONLY: Work Rows (1-2, 1-4, 1-4) once.

ALL SIZES

Shape Armholes (RS): Continuing with Closed Bud Pattern, BO 3 (8, 12, 17) sts at beginning of next 2 rows, 2 sts at beginning of next 0 (4, 6, 8) rows, then decrease 1 st each side every other row 3 (5, 6, 10) times (see Shaping Note)—99 (99, 107, 107) sts remain. Work even through Row 26 of Chart.

Begin Small Arrow Pattern (RS): Change to Small Arrow Pattern from Chart, beginning as indicated in

Chart—83 (83, 89, 89) sts remain after Row 9. Work even through Row 20 of Chart, then repeat Rows 11-20 until armhole measures 8 (8 1/2, 9 1/2, 10)", ending with a WS row.

Shape Shoulders (RS): BO 6 (6, 7, 7) sts at beginning of next 6 rows, then 5 sts at beginning of next 2 rows. BO remaining 37 sts for Back neck.

FRONT
Work as for Back through Row 8. Place markers 46 (57, 68, 79) sts in from each edge.

Begin Closed Bud Pattern (RS): Working waist shaping as for Back, work to first marker, work sts 34-56 of Closed Bud Pattern from Chart to next marker, work to end. Continuing to work waist shaping, and working

The strategic decreases create directional bands of stitches against the solid fabric, making them appear three-dimensional or folded over other areas of stitches.

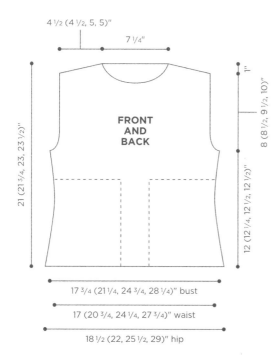

4 1/2 (4 1/2, 5, 5)"
7 1/4"
FRONT AND BACK
1"
8 (8 1/2, 9 1/2, 10)"
21 (21 3/4, 23, 23 1/2)"
12 (12 1/4, 12 1/2, 12 1/2)"
17 3/4 (21 1/4, 24 3/4, 28 1/4)" bust
17 (20 3/4, 24 1/4, 27 3/4)" waist
18 1/2 (22, 25 1/2, 29)" hip

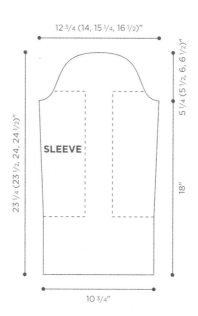

12 3/4 (14, 15 1/4, 16 1/2)"
5 1/4 (5 1/2, 6, 6 1/2)"
SLEEVE
23 1/4 (23 1/2, 24, 24 1/2)"
18"
10 3/4"

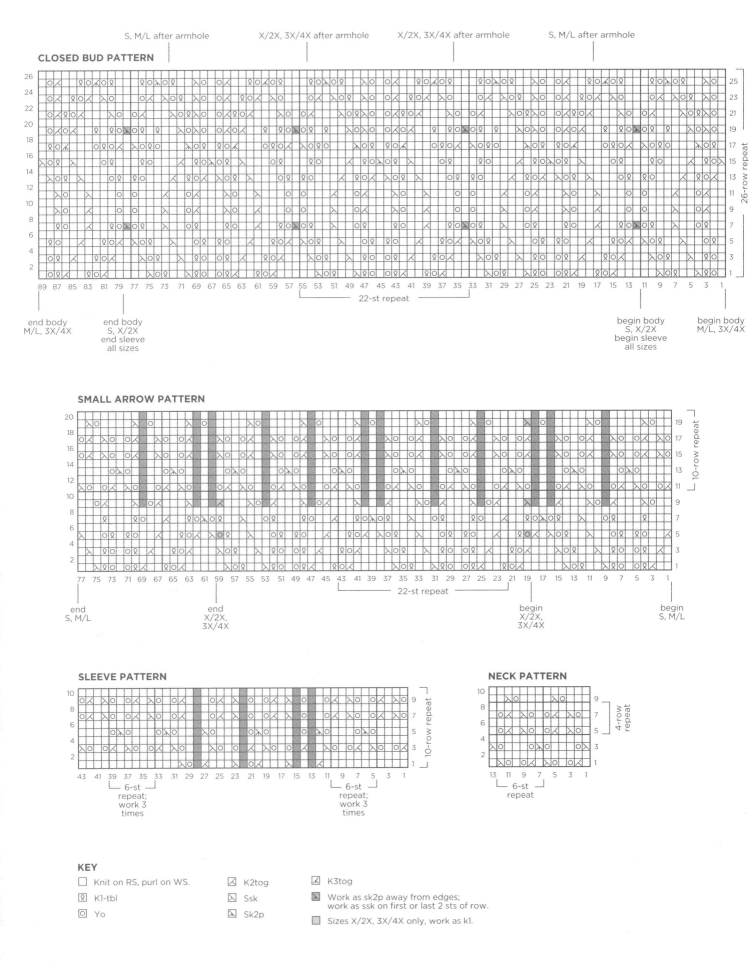

CLOSED BUD PATTERN

S, M/L after armhole

X/2X, 3X/4X after armhole

X/2X, 3X/4X after armhole

S, M/L after armhole

22-st repeat

26-row repeat

end body
M/L, 3X/4X

end body
S, X/2X
end sleeve
all sizes

begin body
S, X/2X
begin sleeve
all sizes

begin body
M/L, 3X/4X

SMALL ARROW PATTERN

22-st repeat

10-row repeat

end
S, M/L

end
X/2X,
3X/4X

begin
X/2X,
3X/4X

begin
S, M/L

SLEEVE PATTERN

6-st
repeat;
work 3
times

6-st
repeat;
work 3
times

10-row repeat

NECK PATTERN

6-st
repeat

4-row
repeat

KEY

☐ Knit on RS, purl on WS.

ℚ K1-tbl

◯ Yo

◿ K2tog

◺ Ssk

⋏ Sk2p

◿ K3tog

◤ Work as sk2p away from edges;
work as ssk on first or last 2 sts of row.

▢ Sizes X/2X, 3X/4X only, work as k1.

center 23 sts in Closed Bud Pattern and remaining sts in St st, work even until 3 vertical repeats of Chart have been completed, ending with a WS row—111 (133, 155, 177) sts.

(RS) Change to Closed Bud Pattern from Chart across all sts. Work as for Back until armhole measures 7 (7 1/2, 8, 8 1/2)", ending with a WS row. Make note of the row of Chart you ended with.

Shape Left Neck Edge: *Note: Neck is shaped using short rows (see Special Techniques, page 154). Shoulder shaping is worked at the same time as neck shaping; please read entire section through before beginning.*

Rows 1 (RS) and 2: Work 31 (31, 34, 34) sts, wrp-t, work to end. Place center 21 neck sts on one holder and 31 (31, 35, 35) right shoulder sts on second holder.

Rows 3-16: Work to 1 st before wrapped st of row before last row, wrp-t, work to end.

AT THE SAME TIME, when armhole measures 8 (8 1/2, 9, 9 1/2)", ending with a WS row, shape shoulder as for Back. Place remaining 8 sts on neck holder. Rejoin yarn to sts on hold for right neck edge; work even for 1 row. Shape right neck edge and shoulder as for left beginning short rows with a RS row.

SLEEVES

Using size US 2 needles and Provisional CO (see Special Techniques, page 154), CO 67 sts. Work as for Back through Row 8.

Begin Closed Bud Pattern (RS): Change to Closed Bud Pattern from Chart, beginning where indicated in Chart. Work even until 2 vertical repeats of Chart have been completed, ending with a WS row.

(RS) K22, pm, work across 23 sts from Chart, pm, knit to end. Continuing to work center 23 sts in Closed Bud Pattern and remaining sts in St st, work even for 1", ending with a WS row.

Shape Sleeve (RS): Increase 1 st each side this row, then every 6 (6, 4, 4) rows 5 (9, 13, 17) times, as follows: K1, M1, work to last st, M1, k1—79 (87, 95,

103) sts. Work even until 6 vertical repeats have been completed from the beginning, ending with a WS row.

Shape Cap (RS): Continuing with pattern as established, BO 3 (8, 12, 17) sts at beginning of next 2 rows, then decrease 1 st each side every other row 3 (2, 2, 1) time(s), as follows: K1, ssk, work to last 3 sts, k2tog, k1—67 sts remain. Work even through Row 8 of Chart.

(RS) Change to Sleeve Pattern from Chart. Work even for 2 rows—63 sts remain.

(RS) Decrease 1 st each side this row, every 4 rows 0 (0, 1, 3) time(s), every other row 13 (17, 16, 16) times, then every row 6 (2, 2, 0) times, as follows: On RS rows, K1, ssk, work to last 3 sts, k2tog, k1; on WS rows, p1, p2tog, work to last 3 sts, p2tog-tbl, p1. BO remaining 23 sts.

FINISHING

Block as desired. Sew right shoulder seam.

Collar: With RS facing, using size US 3 needle, beginning at left front neck edge, pick up and knit 1 st, [k1 from holder, pick up and knit 1 st] 8 times, work in Small Arrow Pattern across center 21 neck sts, beginning with

row following last row worked on Front, pick up and knit 1 st, [k1, pick up and knit 1 st] 8 times, pick up and knit 36 sts from Back neck—91 sts. Working back and forth, purl 1 row.

(RS) Change to Neck Pattern from Chart, beginning with row following last row worked across center Front sts. *Note: Rows 1-10 of Neck Pattern Chart correspond to Rows 11-20 of Small Arrow Pattern Chart.* Work even until Collar measures approximately 1 1/2" from pick-up row, ending with Row 8 of Chart. Repeat Rows 5-8 twice. BO all sts loosely.

Set in Sleeves. Sew side and Sleeve seams.

Button Placket: Sew buttons to left Front shoulder and neck edge, the first beginning 1/2" below neck BO, the last 1/2" from outside edge of shoulder, and the remaining 4 evenly spaced between. Using crochet hook, beginning at Back BO edge of collar, and working toward outside edge of Back shoulder, *work single crochet into each st or row along edge to button, work crochet chain opposite button, making sure chain is long enough to reach around button snugly; repeat from * to last button, work single crochet to end. Fasten off.

art deco leaves cardigan

SIZES

Small (Medium, Large, X-Large)

To fit bust sizes 34-38 (38-42, 42-46, 46-50)

Note: This garment is very stretchy; it fits a range of sizes. If you want a closer-fitting garment, work a size where the upper measurement of the range fits your measurements. If you want a looser-fitting garment, work a size where the lower measurement fits your measurements.

FINISHED MEASUREMENTS

34 (38, 42, 46)" bust, without stretching

YARN

Alchemy Yarns of Transformation Silk Purse (100% silk; 138 yards / 50 grams): 8 (8, 9, 9) hanks #95M Mica for long sleeve version; 7 (8, 8, 9) hanks for 3/4-length version

NEEDLES

One 29" (70 cm) long or longer circular (circ) needle size US 5 (3.75 mm)

Change needle size if necessary to obtain correct gauge.

NOTIONS

Crochet hook size US B/1 (2.25 mm); crochet hook size US F/5 (3.75 mm); waste yarn; stitch markers, including 2 removable stitch markers; stitch holders; six 1" wide hook-and-eye closures

GAUGE

1 repeat of Art Deco Leaves Pattern from Chart = 5⁵/₈" (14 cm) wide x 6" (15 cm) long

NOTES

The Cardigan is begun with a provisional cast-on at the waist, then the Upper Body is worked in one piece to the armholes. The Fronts and Back are divided and worked to the shoulder. The Lower Body is picked up from the provisional cast-on and worked down to the bottom edge. The Sleeves are worked in the same manner.

For the Medium, Large, and X-Large sizes, you will work a filler stitch pattern at the underarm to increase the width of each size without interrupting or changing the flow of the Art Deco Leaves pattern.

SHAPING NOTE

When working shaping for the armholes, neck, and sleeve cap, make sure to keep the Side Panel pattern correct. In other words, if you cannot work a full decrease within the Side Panel pattern (after working the shaping decreases), do not work the yo(s) associated with that decrease in the pattern, and vice versa; work the sts in St st instead.

UPPER BODY

Using Provisional CO (see Special Techniques, page 154), CO 28 sts for Left Front, pm 0 (11, 19, 29) sts for side panel, pm (omit this marker for size Small), 81 sts for Back, pm 0 (11, 19, 29) sts for side panel, pm (omit for size Small), 55 sts for Right Front—164 (186, 202, 222) sts. Purl 1 row.

SIZE SMALL ONLY (RS): K1, work Waist Pattern from Chart to last st, k1.

SIZES MEDIUM AND LARGE ONLY
(RS): K1, work Waist Pattern from Chart to first marker, work Side Panel Chart (A, B, –) to second marker, work Waist Pattern from Chart to third marker, work Side Panel Chart (A, B, –) to fourth marker, work Waist Pattern from Chart to last st, k1.

SIZE X-LARGE ONLY (RS): Slip 1, work Waist Pattern from Chart to first marker, *work Side Panel Chart C over 5 sts, Side Panel Chart B over 19 sts, then Side Panel C* to second marker, work Waist Pattern from Chart to third marker, repeat from * to * to fourth marker, work Waist Pattern from Chart to last st, k1.

ALL SIZES (WS): Slip 1, purl to last st, p1. Work even for 4 rows, slipping the first st of every row.

SIZE SMALL ONLY (RS): Slip 1, work Art Deco Leaves Pattern from Chart to last st, k1.

SIZES MEDIUM, LARGE, AND X-LARGE ONLY (RS): Slip 1, work Art Deco Leaves Pattern from Chart to first marker, work to second marker as established, work Art Deco Leaves Pattern to third marker, work to fourth marker as established, work Art Deco Leaves Pattern to last st, k1.**

ALL SIZES: Work even until piece measures 8 1/2" from the beginning, slipping the first st of every row, and ending with a WS row. Place removable st marker on center st between first and second markers and third and fourth markers (omit for size Small). This will mark the beginning of the armhole edge.

RIGHT FRONT
SIZE SMALL ONLY (RS): Continuing in patterns as established, work to first marker, turn. Place remaining sts on holder. Working on Right Front sts only, work even until armhole measures approximately 6", ending with Row 10 of Art Deco Leaves Pattern.

SIZES MEDIUM, LARGE, AND X-LARGE ONLY (RS): Continuing in patterns as established, work to first armhole (removable) marker, turn; remove marker. Place remaining sts on holder.

Shape Armhole (WS): Continuing in patterns as established, and working on Right Front sts only, BO (2, 3, 7) sts at armhole edge once, then decrease 1 st every other row until (0, 1, 1) st(s) remain(s) between marker and armhole edge, as follows: Work to last 2 sts, k2tog (see Shaping

Leaves paired in opposing columns create diamond-shaped areas filled with lace medallions between their tips. Columns of faggoting serve as branches.

Note). Work even until armhole measures approximately (6, 7, 7)", ending with Row (10, 14, 14) of Art Deco Leaves Pattern.

ALL SIZES

Shape Neck (RS): Continuing in patterns as established, BO 43 (43, 46, 46) sts in pattern at neck edge once, then decrease 1 st every other row 3

4 3/4 (4 3/4, 4 1/2, 4 1/2)"

8 1/4 (8 1/4, 8 3/4, 8 3/4)"

FRONTS AND BACK

provisional cast-on

22 1/2 (23, 23 1/2, 24)"

7 (7 1/2, 8, 8 1/2)"

8 1/2"

7"

31 1/2 (35 1/2, 39 1/2, 43 1/2)" waist

34 (38, 42, 46)" hip and bust

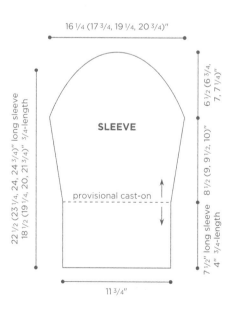

16 1/4 (17 3/4, 19 1/4, 20 3/4)"

SLEEVE

provisional cast-on

22 1/2 (23 1/4, 24, 24 3/4)" long sleeve
18 1/2 (19 1/4, 20, 21 3/4)" 3/4-length

6 1/2 (6 3/4, 7, 7 1/4)"

7 1/2" long sleeve
4" 3/4-length

8 1/2 (9, 9 1/2, 10)"

11 3/4"

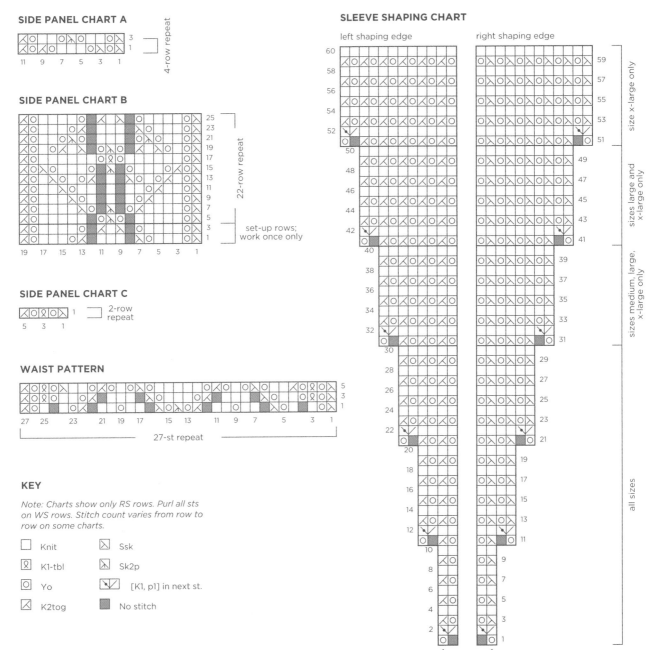

SIDE PANEL CHART A

4-row repeat

11 9 7 5 3 1

3
1

SIDE PANEL CHART B

22-row repeat

set-up rows;
work once only

19 17 15 13 11 9 7 5 3 1

25
23
21
19
17
15
13
11
9
7
5
3
1

SIDE PANEL CHART C

2-row repeat

5 3 1

1

WAIST PATTERN

27 25 23 21 19 17 15 13 11 9 7 5 3 1

5
3
1

27-st repeat

SLEEVE SHAPING CHART

left shaping edge   right shaping edge

size x-large only

sizes large and
x-large only

sizes medium, large,
x-large only

all sizes

KEY

*Note: Charts show only RS rows. Purl all sts
on WS rows. Stitch count varies from row to
row on some charts.*

☐ Knit   ⊠ Ssk

⊠ K1-tbl   ⊠ Sk2p

○ Yo   ⊠ [K1, p1] in next st.

⊠ K2tog   ▨ No stitch

ART DECO LEAVES PATTERN

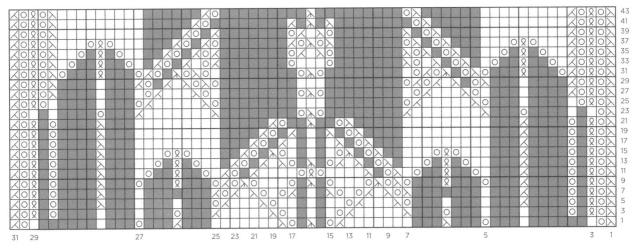

times, as follows: Slip 1, ssk, work to end—25 (25, 26, 26) sts remain. Work even until armhole measures 7 (7 1/2, 8, 8 1/2)", ending with a WS row. Make note of which row of the Chart you end on; you will end the Back and Left Front on the same row. Place remaining sts on holder.

BACK

SIZE SMALL ONLY (RS): Rejoin yarn to sts on holder. Continuing in patterns as established, work to first marker, turn. Place remaining sts on holder.

SIZES MEDIUM, LARGE, AND X-LARGE ONLY

Shape Armhole (RS): Continuing in patterns as established, and working on Back sts only, BO (2, 3, 7) sts, work to st before armhole (removable) marker, turn. Place remaining sts on holder.

(WS) BO (2, 3, 7) sts, work to end.

(RS) Decrease 1 st each side every other row until (0, 1, 1) st(s) remain(s) between marker and armhole edge, as follows: Ssk, work to last 2 sts, k2tog.

ALL SIZES: Work even until armhole measures approximately 7 (7 1/2, 8, 8 1/2)", ending with same row of Art Deco Leaves Pattern as for Right Front. Place remaining sts on holder.

LEFT FRONT

SIZE SMALL ONLY (RS): Rejoin yarn to sts on holder.

SIZES MEDIUM, LARGE, AND X-LARGE ONLY

Shape Armhole (RS): Rejoin yarn to sts on holder. Continuing in patterns as established, BO (2, 3, 7) sts at armhole edge once, then decrease 1 st at armhole edge every other row until (0, 1, 1) st(s) remain(s) between marker and armhole edge, as follows: Ssk, work to end.

ALL SIZES: Work even until armhole measures approximately 6 (6, 7, 7)", ending with Row 11 (11, 15, 15) of Art Deco Leaves Pattern.

ALL SIZES

Shape Neck (WS): Continuing in pattern as established, BO 6 sts in pattern at neck edge once, then decrease 1 st every other row 3 times, as follows: Work to last 3 sts, k2tog, k1—25 (25, 26, 26) sts remain. Work even until armhole measures 7 (7 1/2, 8, 8 1/2)", ending with same row of Art Deco Leaves Pattern as for Right Front. Place remaining sts on holder.

LOWER BODY

With RS facing, transfer sts from waste yarn to needle, placing markers as at CO for Upper Body. With WS facing, rejoin yarn at Right Front and purl 1 WS row. Work as for Upper Body from ** to **.

ALL SIZES: Work Rows 1-44 of Art Deco Leaves Pattern once, then work Rows 1-8 once.

BO Row (RS): Using smaller crochet hook and referring to Row 9 of Art Deco Leaves Pattern Chart (or next row of Side Panel Chart when working across side panels) as you work, BO all sts using Crochet Chain BO, as follows: *Insert hook from right to left through next 2 sts at once (or 3 sts if Chart shows sk2p), and work single crochet, chain 6; repeat from * to last 2 sts, single crochet into last 2 sts. Fasten off.

Using Kitchener st (see Special Techniques, page 155), graft Left Front shoulder sts to the same number of sts on the left Back. Repeat for the Right Front shoulder. With RS facing, rejoin yarn to remaining Back sts. BO all sts loosely.

UPPER SLEEVES

Using Provisional CO, CO 68 sts. Purl 1 row.

(RS) Slip 1, work Art Deco Leaves Pattern from Chart to last st, k1.

(WS) Slip 1, work to last st, p1. Work even for 4 rows.

Shape Sleeves (RS): Slip 1, work right shaping edge of Sleeve Shaping Chart, work Art Deco Leaves Pattern to last st, work left shaping edge of Sleeve Shaping Chart, k1—70 sts.

Work even, working Charts as established, until 30 (40, 50, 60) rows of Sleeve Shaping Chart have been completed—80 (84, 88, 92) sts. Work even until piece measures 8 1/2 (9, 9 1/2, 10)" from the beginning, ending with a WS row.

Shape Cap (RS): BO 2 sts at the beginning of the next 12 rows, then decrease 1 st each side every other row until 22 (24, 26, 28) sts remain, as follows: K1, ssk, work to last 2 sts, k2tog, k1. BO all sts.

LOWER SLEEVES

With WS facing, transfer sts from waste yarn to needle. Rejoin yarn and purl 1 row.

(RS) Slip 1, work Art Deco Leaves Pattern from Chart to last st, k1.

(WS) Slip 1, work to last st, p1. Work Rows 3-30 of Chart once for 3/4-length Sleeve, or Rows 3-44, then Rows 1-8 for long Sleeve.

BO Row (RS): Using smaller crochet hook and Crochet Chain BO, and referring to Row 31 of Art Deco Leaves Pattern Chart for 3/4-length Sleeve or Row 9 for long Sleeve, BO all sts as for Lower Body.

FINISHING

Set in Sleeves. Sew Sleeve seams.

Crochet Edging: With RS facing, using larger crochet hook, beginning at bottom edge of Left Front, work Crab Stitch Edging (see Special Techniques, page 155) up Left Front, around neck, down Right Front, then back again. Fasten off.

Sew hook portions of closures to Right Front, 1/4" in from center Front edge, the first just below the neck shaping, the last beginning 5 1/2" above the bottom edge, and the remaining 4 evenly spaced between. Sew eye portions to Left Front, opposite hooks.

DOILIES

Vintage Lace in New Directions

IN THIS FINAL CHAPTER I HAVE APPLIED MY OWN DESIGN CONCEPTS AND silhouettes to a specific vintage lace genre: doily knitting or *Kunststricken*. This form of lace knitting seems to stem from the circular knit bonnet backs of earlier centuries, which were worked in the round from the center outward. This style flourished in Europe in the 1930s and '40s and has become an (often secret) obsession of many a serious knitter ever since. Traditionally worked in stiff cotton thread, doily patterns existed in various sizes and shapes to dress every household surface, from coasters and placemats, to smaller tea table covers and elaborate tablecloths. These items were usually blocked and starched and featured a crochet loop bind off that could be stretched on pins. The stitchwork on these doilies is truly astounding. Herbert Niebling and other designers of the era, greatly influenced by the Bauhaus and Arts and Crafts movements, were quite adept at manipulating the solid and open areas and imitating various floral motifs drawn from other textiles, such as Valenciennes lace. Part of the beauty of these doilies is in their arrangement: The pattern builds out from the center and increases within wedge- or pinwheel-shaped segments to build a flat circle, octagon, pentagon, or other roundish shape. The overall effect is often kaleidoscopic, appearing as reflected foliage or highlighting geometric relationships that are typically found in nature.

In these projects, I explore how doily segments can be translated into a less delicate scale or utilized in isolation for garments and accessories. There are many tubular areas of our bodies that require garments with a rate of increase, and doily motifs can easily be sampled and manipulated to suit this purpose. For instance, a wedge of a doily is crafted to drape over shoulders of the Bell Sleeve Blouse (page 144), and two pattern wedges placed center front become the neckline of the Thistle Bodice (page 136). And instead of working in fine thread, as was traditionally used for doily knitting, I have opted for heavier yarn in the Sunflower Satchel (page 132) in order to enjoy the stitch pattern at a zoomed-in scale. Vintage doily stitchwork has a very distinguished character and it is rewarding to be able to give it new form in modern knitwear.

sunflower satchel

This satchel utilizes a small section of a stitch pattern featured in a tablecloth in Marianne Kinzel's *First Book of Modern Lace Knitting*. In her circular tablecloth, which is essentially a large doily, pointed columns delineated with openwork chevrons radiate from a leafy center. I isolated two of these "rays" and then shifted them so that a full column is centered with a half column to each side. By shifting the chevron-bordered motif, the openwork has more impact—especially at this zoomed-in scale. The diagonal lines resemble stems that expand and bloom into a sort of flower towards the base of the bag. What I most admire about Kinzel's doilies is the stylized merging of geometric shapes within a botanical theme—they are streamlined and ornate all at once.

>> See pattern on page 132.

ladybird cravat and hat

Ladybird, a fancy name for ladybug, was a common ground and filler stitch in mid-century doilies. The repeat is easy to follow, relying on alternating triads and single stitches that are gathered into double decreases, creating starlike spots. For these accessories, I've stacked the stitch chart with built-in increases that form a spatula-shaped flounce. The hat, worked from the top down, is essentially two flounces ending with a ribbed brim; the cravat ends with a single flounce and is bound off with crocheted loops (a common doily technique). Chunky Bakelite buttons lend lots of personality to this quirky set.

>> See pattern on page 134.

thistle bodice

When I saw the cover of Marianne Kinzel's *Second Book of Modern Lace Knitting*, I fell in love with the Balmoral Doily pictured there. That doily features stemmed globes ringing its center, which I first thought to be pomegranate fruits, but upon reading the introduction discovered to be thistles (the symbol of Scotland). As I studied the photograph, I came to realize that I was interested not just in the thistle motif, but also the calyx (the group of serrated leaves at the base of the bloom). At the outer circumference of Kinzel's doily, these branch out with their flamelike tips forming little cups of spiky lace. These cup shapes reminded me of a brassiere, and so I got the idea to work a bodice from the top down beginning with a thistle calyx at the top of each breast. Increases are made at each side until the back is joined, and then the bodice is worked circularly to the hem. Laceweight hemp lends thistlelike texture and corsetlike structure to this top, but then softens with washing and has the strength to wear for years.

>> *See pattern on page 136.*

sunray medallion tunic

This tunic was inspired by a goth-chic look from Jean Paul Gaultier—a chunky knit tunic with a cameo portrait printed on a fabric center, worn by a brooding model. Here, I've used the very center of a vintage doily, a sunray medallion, and worked outward from the center; then I used the same sequence for both the sleeves and the skirt. The sunray or sunburst pattern is a traditional quilt motif, especially for quilts given to a bride. In fact, the sunray motif was often carved on a wooden hope chest that would be filled with linens in preparation for marriage. In the knitted version of this motif, the rays of the sun begin at the center of the piece and are delineated by ladder stitch—a simple faggoting pattern.

>> *See pattern on page 140.*

bell sleeve blouse

Vintage doily patterns normally feature charts in wedges, representing one segment of a circle; they have a severe rate of increase because, worked from center point to large border circumference, they need to create a flat rather than domed piece. The potential of the wedge shape was not lost on me. I realized that a doily segment could be perfect for working a bell-shaped sleeve from the narrow sleeve cap down. One could select among many doily charts to create customized sleeves—simply begin above the center of the chart and find a repeat of a few inches. To determine the length of the section, subtract half of the cast-on width where the cap will be sewn to the armhole, filling in the armhole depth. I designed a simple fine-knit tank in cotton crochet thread which will work well with a variety of sleeve patterns. For these winglike sleeves, I have created a variation on a small part of one of Niebling's charts, which is worked flat.

>> *See pattern on page 144.*

hug-me-tight cardigan

In the past decade we've seen a revival of knitted shrugs. They are usually easier to make than most cardigans and are also very flattering and practical. Knitting patterns of the nineteenth century included several clever shrug cardigan styles composed of simple rectangles in stretchable stitch patterns that were then folded and sewn to fit the body—among these are the hug-me-tight, the fit-well, and the emigrant's vest. I've recreated the hug-me-tight here, which is notable for its wide band that hugs the body when buttoned, creating front lapels. The resulting garment is reminiscent of Dior's New Look, with generous proportions on top and a fitted waist.

The large rectangle of a hug-me-tight is an opportunity to work in any combination of lace patterns. For this one I sampled small areas of several vintage doily patterns at random and created a unique lace sequence. As doily motifs are worked in a ring outward with increases built into the motifs, I had to straighten the motifs by adding corresponding decreases to my chart and sometimes had to remove the increase of the original pattern. Being made up of these uncommon altered motifs, the grouping has a novel "sampled" appearance.

>> *See pattern on page 148.*

palm leaf wrap

The cultivation of tropical plants, especially in glass and iron hothouses, were a craze in Victorian England, and among the ones still in existence is the magnificent Palm House at Kew Gardens in London. From the mid-nineteenth to the mid-twentieth century, palm leaves were also popular in textile prints, flaunting the opulence and exoticism of the natural world; plus, the plumed, shell-like shape of the palm leaf lends itself well to graphic arrangement. I was very attracted to a palmlike motif in a large doily by Herbert Niebling. I admired how open the fronds become as the doily is worked outward; with lace done every round, it gives the base an almost horizontal slant. I figured out a method to adopt the motif for a flat piece without losing the exotic openwork. I chose a heavier yarn to blow up the proportion and then I bound off each frond separately to further enhance the sculptural effect.

>> See pattern on page 152 .

sunflower satchel

FINISHED MEASUREMENTS

22 1/2" wide at widest point x 17" high, not including handles

YARN

Loop-d-Loop by Teva Durham New Birch (65% cotton / 35% silk; 98 yards / 50 grams): 5 balls #13 Maize

NEEDLES

One 29" (70 cm) long or longer circular (circ) needle size US 7 (4.5 mm)

Change needle size if necessary to obtain correct gauge.

NOTIONS

One pair slatted wooden purse handles 11-13" wide at base [such as Sunbelt Fastener Co. item W03-N 12" natural wood]; 1 yard

lining fabric (in a shade and pattern that will not distract from the lace pattern, but will subtly enhance the ability to see it); thread to match lining; sewing machine or sewing needle

GAUGE

14 sts and 24 rows = 4" (10 cm) in Lace Pattern from Chart

FRONT AND BACK (both alike)

CO 49 sts. Purl 1 row. Begin Lace Pattern from Chart. Work through st 25, then work in reverse, beginning with st 24 and working back to st 1, reversing all k2togs and ssks, but not sk2ps; work even until entire Chart is complete, ending with a WS row—79 sts. Change to St st, beginning with a knit row. Work even for 3 rows. BO all sts.

GUSSET (make 2)

CO 7 sts.

Row 1 (WS): Purl.

Row 2: K2, yo, sk2p, yo, k2.

Repeat Rows 1 and 2 eight times. Purl 1 row. Begin Gusset pattern from Chart, working sts and rows outlined in red, and ending with a WS row. Change to St st, beginning with a knit row. Work even for 3 rows. BO all sts.

FINISHING

Block pieces lightly. Sew BO edges of Front and Back together. Cut piece of lining fabric the same size and shape as the sewn Front/Back, plus 1/2" seam allowance along all edges. Cut 2 pieces of lining fabric the same size and shape as the Gussets, plus 1/2" seam allowance along all edges. Sew BO edge of knitted Gusset to side edges of knitted Front and Back, centering BO edge of Gusset on bottom seam (see schematic). Sew remaining side edges of Gusset to sides of Front and Back, then continue up side seams of Front and Back. Sew lining as for Satchel, with all the seams to the WS, making sure to finish off seams neatly so that no raw edges show through lace of Satchel. Attach one handle to each side, as follows: Center handle over CO edge. With 2 strands of yarn held together, using tapestry needle, sew handle to CO edge, working into each edge stitch then over the handle slat twice to completely cover handle below slat (see photo, page 124). With WSs of Satchel and lining together, sew top edge of lining to top edge of Satchel.

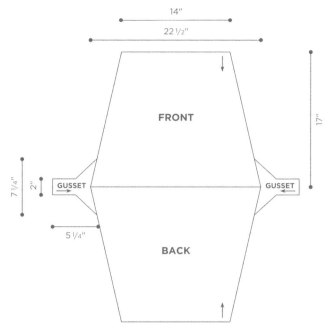

Shifting outward from strong braided openwork lines, dual branches of 6-stitch openwork diamond motif reminiscent of Madeira lace move on the diagonal and meet to form chevrons and solid petal-shaped areas.

LACE PATTERN

Notes: Chart shows only RS rows. Purl all sts on WS rows. Chart shows only right half of Satchel; for left half, Chart is worked in mirror image. Work Chart to st 25, then work Chart backward, beginning with st 24 and working back to st 1; reverse single-st decreases, working ssk for k2tog and vice versa. Do not reverse double decreases; work them as sk2p on both halves.

KEY

☐	Knit	◿	K2tog	▨	No stitch	
○	Yo	◺	Ssk	☐	Gusset pattern	
⊠	K1-tbl	⋏	Sk2p			

ladybird cravat and hat

STITCH PATTERN

1x1 Rib

(odd number of sts; 2-row repeat)

Row 1 (WS): Slip 1, *p1, k1; repeat from * to end.

Row 2: Slip 1, *k1, p1; repeat from * to end.

Repeat Rows 1 and 2 for 1x1 Rib.

Cravat

CO 9 sts. Begin 1x1 Rib; work even until piece measures 22 (24)", or to desired length around neck (button should nestle at collar bone).

Next Row (RS): Begin Ladybird Pattern from Chart; work even until entire Chart is complete.

BO Row (WS): Slip 1 st to crochet hook, chain 5, *single crochet into next st on needle, chain 5; repeat from * to last st, slip st in last st to join. Fasten off.

FINISHING

Block piece lightly. Sew button to center of ribbing on RS, 1/2" above CO edge. To wear, push button from back to front through purl st approximately 1" above beginning of lace pattern.

SIZES

Cravat: Small/Medium (Large/X-Large)
Hat: One size

FINISHED MEASUREMENTS

Cravat: 20 1/2 (22 1/2)" around neck, buttoned
Hat: 19" circumference
Note: Hat can stretch easily.

YARN

Cravat: Loop-d-Loop by Teva Durham Granite (95% wool/5% nylon; 55 yards / 50 grams): 1 ball #001 Quartz
Hat: Loop-d-Loop by Teva Durham Granite (95% wool/5% nylon; 55 yards / 50 grams): 1 ball #001 Quartz

NEEDLES

Cravat: One pair straight needles size US 13 (9 mm)
Hat: One pair straight needles size US 13 (9 mm)
One pair straight needles size US 10 (6 mm)
Change needle size if necessary to obtain correct gauge.

NOTIONS

Cravat: Crochet hook size J/10 (6 mm); one 1 1/4" button
Hat: Two 1" buttons

GAUGE

8 sts and 10 rows = 4" (10 cm) in Stockinette stitch (St st), using larger needles

Hat

Note: Hat is worked from the top down.

Using larger needles, CO 6 sts. Purl 1 row.

(RS) *[K1, p1, k1] into next st; repeat from * to end—18 sts. Purl 1 row.

(RS) Begin Ladybird Pattern from Chart; work Rows 1-13 once—38 sts.

Purl 1 row, increase 1 st at end of row—39 sts.

Change to 1x1 Rib; work even for 2". BO all sts loosely. Cut yarn, leaving 12" tail for sewing side seam.

FINISHING

Using tail, sew side seam to top of Hat, then thread yarn through CO sts to close hole at top of Hat.

Button Strap: Using smaller needles, CO 5 sts. Begin 1x1 Rib; work even until piece measures 3" from the beginning. BO all sts.

Sew 1 button 1/2" from CO end and 1 button 1/2" from BO end, centered in ribbing. Sew Strap to side of Hat, with CO edge at seam.

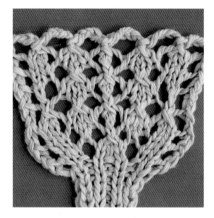

Yarnovers alternate with double decreases (sk2p) every fourth row, creating a filigree effect.

LADYBIRD PATTERN

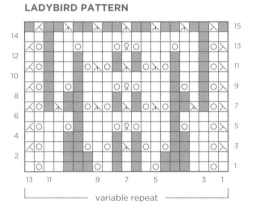

KEY

□	Knit on RS, purl on WS.
○	Yo
ℓ	K1-tbl
⊿	K2tog
⊼	Ssk
⋏	Sk2p
▨	No stitch

thistle bodice

SIZES

Small (Medium, Large, X-Large)

To fit bust sizes 30-34 (34-38, 38-42, 42-46)"

Note: This garment is meant to fit closely. If you want a looser-fitting garment, work a size where the lower measurement of the range fits your measurements.

FINISHED MEASUREMENTS

29 1/4 (33 1/2, 37 1/2, 41 3/4)" bust

YARN

Lanaknits Designs Allhemp3 (100% hemp; 165 yards / 50 grams): 3 (4, 5, 5) hanks #010 Pearl

NEEDLES

Two 24" (60 cm) long circular (circ) needles size US 2 (2.75 mm)

Change needle size if necessary to obtain correct gauge.

NOTIONS

Crochet hook size US B/1 (2.5 mm); stitch markers

GAUGE

23 sts and 36 rows = 4" (10 cm) in Ladybird Stitch from Chart, after blocking

RIGHT BUST

Note: Piece is worked from the top down.

CO 5 sts. Begin Bust Pattern from Chart; work even through Row 25—41 sts. Cut yarn and leave sts on needle.

LEFT BUST

CO 5 sts. Begin Bust Pattern from Chart, beginning with st 5 and working in reverse to st 1, reversing all sts except sk2ps and k3togs; work even through Row 25—41 sts. Do not cut yarn.

BODICE TOP

(WS) Work across Left Bust, CO 1 st (this will become center front st marked on Chart), work across Right Bust, working all sts onto one needle—83 sts. Work even, continuing to work Chart across Right and Left Busts as established, and working center st as indicated on Chart, until you have completed Row 44 of Chart. Work Rows 37-44 once more, then work Rows 37-43 once more—99 sts.

BODY

(WS) Work to last 2 sts, pm, k2, CO 17 (41, 65, 89) sts for center back—116 (140, 164, 188) sts. Place marker on center front st.

(RS) Join for working in the rnd. Slip 2 sts from right-hand needle to left-hand needle; pm for beginning of rnd. Knit to first marker, work in Ladybird Stitch from Chart to 3 sts before center marked st, k2, yo, [k1, p1, k1] into 1 st, yo, k1-tbl (center marked st), yo, [k1, p1, k1] into 1 st, yo, k2, work in Ladybird Stitch to end, ending with st 3 of Chart—168 (192, 216, 240) sts.

Next Rnd: Purl to next marker, work Rnd 2 of Ladybird Stitch from Chart to end.

Next Rnd: Work Rnd 3 of Ladybird Stitch across all sts, beginning with st 4 of Chart. Work even for 15 rnds, ending with Rnd 2 of Chart, and ending 2 sts before beginning of rnd marker on last rnd.

Next Rnd: Change to Arrowhead Pattern from Chart, beginning with st 1 (11, 1, 11) of Chart. Work even until entire Chart is complete—147 (168, 189, 210) sts remain. Repeat Rnds

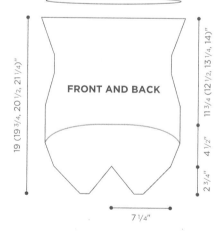

41 (46 3/4, 52 3/4 58 1/2)" hip

27 1/2 (31 1/2, 35 1/4, 39 1/4)" waist

29 1/4 (33 1/2, 37 1/2, 41 3/4)" bust

19 (19 3/4, 20 1/2, 21 1/4)"

FRONT AND BACK

11 3/4 (12 1/2, 13 1/4, 14)"

4 1/2"

2 3/4"

7 1/4"

Note: Piece is worked from the top down.

41-44 four (5, 7, 8) times. *Note: If you wish to adjust the length of the Bodice, you may do so at this point by working more or fewer repeats of Rnds 41-44. You will add or subtract approximately 1/2" (blocked) for every 4 rnds you add or subtract. Make sure you end with Rnd 44.*

Next Rnd: Change to Hip Pattern from Chart, beginning with st 13 (1, 13, 1) of Chart. Work even through Rnd 32 of Chart. Using crochet hook, work crochet trim at end of Chart, working single crochet into backs of number of sts shown on Chart, followed by chain 8. Work in this manner around entire bottom edge, join with slip st to beginning of rnd. Fasten off.

SHOULDER STRAPS (make 2)
CO 5 sts.

All Rows: K2, yo, k2tog, k1. Work even until piece measures 15" from the beginning. Leave sts on needle. Sew CO edge of each Strap to CO edge of each Bust. Try piece on and adjust length of Straps if necessary. BO all sts. Sew BO edge to CO sts for center back, spacing Straps comfortably.

FINISHING
Block piece, pinning crochet chain edge out to points.

Many textures of lace evolve in this pattern. The waist is defined by a berrylike pattern done with staggered decreases and increases. The bodice begins and ends in Ladybird stitch, a complex-looking mesh that is easily done by alternating between rows of yarnovers with three stitches and single twisted stitches, and rows of yarnovers and double decreases. A crocheted edge also emphasizes the Ladybird mesh stitch grouping.

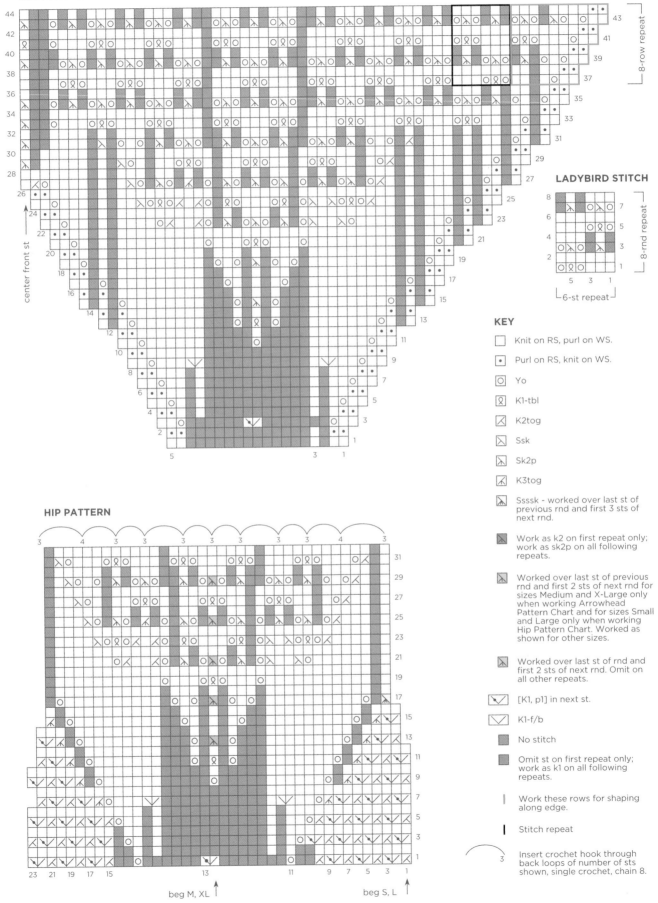

BUST PATTERN

center front st

LADYBIRD STITCH

8-rnd repeat

6-st repeat

KEY

☐	Knit on RS, purl on WS.
•	Purl on RS, knit on WS.
O	Yo
℧	K1-tbl
⟋	K2tog
⟍	Ssk
⋏	Sk2p
⫽	K3tog
	Ssssk - worked over last st of previous rnd and first 3 sts of next rnd.
▨	Work as k2 on first repeat only; work as sk2p on all following repeats.
	Worked over last st of previous rnd and first 2 sts of next rnd for sizes Medium and X-Large only when working Arrowhead Pattern Chart and for sizes Small and Large only when working Hip Pattern Chart. Worked as shown for other sizes.
	Worked over last st of rnd and first 2 sts of next rnd. Omit on all other repeats.
⋁	[K1, p1] in next st.
⋁	K1-f/b
▨	No stitch
▨	Omit st on first repeat only; work as k1 on all following repeats.
❘	Work these rows for shaping along edge.
❘	Stitch repeat
⌒ 3	Insert crochet hook through back loops of number of sts shown, single crochet, chain 8.

HIP PATTERN

beg M, XL

beg S, L

ARROWHEAD PATTERN

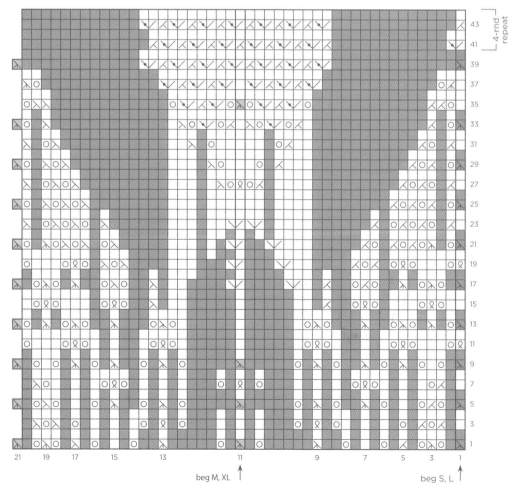

sunray medallion tunic

SIZES
Small/Medium (Large, X-Large)

FINISHED MEASUREMENTS
38 ½ (41 ½, 44 ½)" bust

YARN
Blue Sky Alpacas Worsted Hand Dyes (50% royal alpaca / 50% merino wool; 100 grams / 100 yards): 8 (9, 9) hanks #2006 Black

NEEDLES
Two 29" (70 cm) long circular (circ) needles size US 10 ½ (6.5 mm)
Change needle size if necessary to obtain correct gauge.

NOTIONS
Crochet hook size US H/8 (5 mm); stitch markers; stitch holders

GAUGE
12 sts and 16 rows = 4" (10 cm) in Stockinette stitch (St st)

NOTES

The Tunic is begun with two Medallions; the Medallions form the top section of the Front and Back. The two ribbed Side Panels and two Sleeves are then worked from the top down. The pieces are assembled, then the Peplum is picked up from the bottom of the Medallions and Side Panels and worked down.

When working the Medallions, you will work with two circular needles. One needle will hold the stitches, while you work the stitches with the second needle.

You may work the Medallion and the Sleeves from the written pattern or the Chart.

STITCH PATTERNS

1x1 Rib
(multiple of 2 sts; 1-row/rnd repeat)

Row/Rnd 1: *K1, p1; repeat from * to end (end k1 if an odd number of sts).

Row/Rnd 2: Knit the knit sts and purl the purl sts as they face you.

Repeat Row/Rnd 2 for 1x1 Rib.

2x2 Rib
(multiple of 4 sts; 1-row/rnd repeat)

Row/Rnd 1 (RS): *K2, p2; repeat from * to end (end k2 if working in rows).

Row/Rnd 2: Knit the knit sts and purl the purl sts as they face you.

Repeat Row/Rnd 2 for 2x2 Rib.

MEDALLION PATTERN

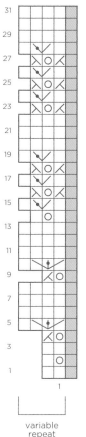

KEY

Note: Medallion is worked in rnds; read all rnds from right to left. Sleeves are worked in rows; only WS row numbers are shown.

☐	Knit
Ⓞ	Yo
⧄	K2tog on RS, p2tog on WS.
⧅	Ssk on RS, p2tog-tbl on WS.
▽	On RS rows, k1, p1, k1 into same st to increase to 3 sts; on WS rows, p1, k1, p1 into same st.
▽	On RS rows, k1, p1 into same st to increase to 2 sts; on WS rows, p1, k1 into same st.
▨	Worked as first or last st on Sleeve only; omit when working Medallion.

MEDALLION (make 2)

Using crochet hook, chain 5, join with slip st to form ring, then transfer st to needle. Using same needle, pick up and knit 7 sts in middle of ring—8 sts. Join for working in the rnd; place marker (pm) for beginning of rnd. Begin Medallion Pattern from text below or from Chart; work even through Rnd 31 of Pattern.

Rnds 1 and 3: Knit.

Rnd 2: *Yo, k1; repeat from * to end— 16 sts.

Rnd 4: *Yo, k2tog; repeat from * to end.

Rnd 5: *[K1, p1, k1] in next st, k1; repeat from * to end—32 sts.

Rnds 6-8: Knit.

Rnd 9: Repeat Rnd 4.

Rnd 10: Repeat Rnd 5—64 sts.

Rnds 11-13: Knit.

Rnd 14: *K1, yo, k1; repeat from * to end—96 sts.

Rnds 15, 17, 19, 24, and 26: *K1, [k1, p1] in next st, k1; repeat from * to end— 128 sts.

Rnds 16, 18, 23, 25, and 27: *K2tog, yo, ssk; repeat from * to end—96 sts remain.

Rnds 20-22: Knit.

Rnd 28: Repeat Rnd 15—128 sts.

Rnds 29-31: Knit.

Shape Medallion into Square: *Note: Medallion will be shaped using short rows (see Special Techniques, page 154).* You'll work short rows at the beginning of the first needle, then at the end of the first needle. Then you'll repeat the process for the second needle. Divide sts between 2 circs (64 sts each). Continuing in St st, and

Working three stitches into each yarnover creates large, round eyelets in the middle of the circular piece. The stranded rungs that bridge the columns above the circle are created by working two stitches and paired decreases into each yarnover.

working back and forth, work short rows at beginning of first needle only as follows:

Rows 1 and 2: Work 16 sts, wrp-t; work to end.

Rows 3 and 4: Work 12 sts, wrp-t; work to end.

Rows 5 and 6: Work 8 sts, wrp-t; work to end.

Rows 7 and 8: Work 4 sts, wrp-t; work to end.

Knit to end of first needle, working wraps together with wrapped sts as you come to them; turn. Repeat short-row shaping at this end of first needle, beginning with a WS row. Repeat for both ends of second needle. BO all sts on both needles, working wraps together with wrapped sts as you come to them. Place marker (A) either side of center 14 sts from first needle, then pm (B) 20 sts to either side of center markers; you will sew the Sleeve caps between these markers. Place marker (C) either side of center 32 sts from second needle; you will pick up Peplum sts from these marked sts.

SIDE PANEL (make 2)
CO 9 (15, 21) sts. Begin 1x1 Rib; work even for 5", ending with a WS row.

Shape Panel (RS): Increase 1 st each side this row, then every 8 rows once, as follows, working increased sts in pattern as they become available:

Work 1, yrn, work to last st, yrn, work 1—13 (19, 25) sts. Work even until piece measures 9 1/2" from the beginning, ending with a WS row, decrease 1 st on last row—12 (18, 24) sts remain. Transfer sts to holder.

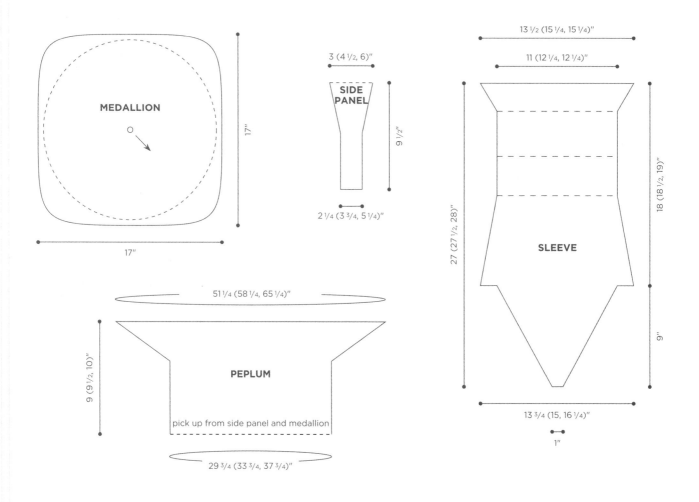

MEDALLION

17"

17"

SIDE PANEL

3 (4 1/2, 6)"

9 1/2"

2 1/4 (3 3/4, 5 1/4)"

PEPLUM

51 1/4 (58 1/4, 65 1/4)"

9 (9 1/2, 10)"

pick up from side panel and medallion

29 3/4 (33 3/4, 37 3/4)"

13 1/2 (15 1/4, 15 1/4)"

11 (12 1/4, 12 1/4)"

SLEEVE

27 (27 1/2, 28)"

18 (18 1/2, 19)"

9"

13 3/4 (15, 16 1/4)"

1"

SLEEVES

CO 3 sts. Begin Medallion Pattern from text below or from Chart; work even through Row 31 of Pattern.

Shape Cap

Rows 1 and 3 (WS): Purl.

Row 2: K1, *yo, k1; repeat from * to end—5 sts.

Row 4: K1, *yo, k2tog; repeat from * to end.

Row 5: *P1, [p1, k1, p1] in next st; repeat from * to last st, p1—9 sts.

Rows 6 and 8: Knit.

Row 7: Purl.

Row 9: *P2tog, yo; repeat from * to last st, p1.

Row 10: K1, *[k1, p1, k1] in next st, k1; repeat from * to end—17 sts.

Rows 11 and 13: Purl.

Row 12: Knit.

Row 14: K1, *k1, yo, k1; repeat from * to end—25 sts.

Rows 15, 17, and 19: *P1, [p1, k1] in next st, p1; repeat from * to last st, p1—33 sts.

Rows 16 and 18: K1, *k2tog, yo, ssk; repeat from * to end—25 sts remain.

Rows 20 and 22: Knit.

Row 21: Purl.

Rows 23, 25, and 27: *P2tog-tbl, yo, p2tog; repeat from * to last st, p1—25 sts remain.

Rows 24, 26, and 28: K1, *k1, [k1, p1] in next st, k1; repeat from * to end—33 sts.

Row 29: Purl.

Row 30: Knit.

Row 31: Purl.

(RS) Change to St st; work even until piece measures 9″ from the beginning, ending with a WS row.

Shape Armholes (RS): CO 4 (6, 8) sts at beginning of next 2 rows—41 (45, 49) sts. Work even until piece measures 2″ from armhole shaping, ending with a WS row.

Shape Sleeve (RS): Decrease 1 st each side this row, then every 6 (6, 4) rows 3 (3, 5) times, as follows: K1, k2tog, knit to last 3 sts, ssk, k1—33 (37, 37) sts remain. Work even until piece measures 8 (8 1/2, 9)″ from armhole shaping, ending with a WS row, increase 1 st at beginning of last row—34 (38, 38) sts.

(RS) Change to 2x2 Rib; work even for 3 1/2″, ending with a WS row, decrease 1 st on last row—33 (37, 37) sts remain.

(RS) *Work Rows 16 and 17 of Medallion Pattern (from text above or from Chart) 3 times, then Rows 20-22 once; repeat from * once.

Shape Cuff (RS): K5, *[yo] 3 times, k4; repeat from * to end.

(WS) *P4, [k1, p1, k1] (1 st in each yo); repeat from * to last 5 sts, p5—54 (61, 61) sts. Work even in St st for 3 rows.

(WS) Change to 1x1 Rib; work even for 1 row. BO all sts in pattern.

FINISHING

Block as desired. Sew Sleeve seam. Leaving center 14 Medallion sts open for neck, sew Sleeve cap to Medallion between center (A) and side (B) markers. Sew CO sts of Side Panel to armhole sts of Sleeve. Sew side edges of Side Panels to Medallion, between Sleeve cap and markers (C) for Peplum pick-up, leaving 32 sts at bottom of Medallion for Peplum, and leaving last st on bottom row of either side of Side Panels unsewn for Peplum.

Peplum: Rejoin yarn at Side Panel. Work in 2x2 Rib across 12 (18, 24) sts of Side Panel, pick up and knit 32 sts across bottom of Front Medallion between C markers, work in 2x2 Rib across 12 (18, 24) sts of Side Panel, pick up and knit 32 sts across bottom of Back Medallion between C markers—88 (100, 112) sts.

Next Rnd: Begin 2x2 Rib; work even for 2 1/2 (3, 3 1/2)″. K1, reposition beginning of rnd marker to after this st.

Next Rnd: Work Rnds 16-28 of Medallion Pattern from Medallion text or from Chart.

Knit 3 Rnds.

Next Rnd: *K4, [yo] 3 times; repeat from * to end.

Next Rnd: *K4, [k1, p1, k1] (1 st in each yo); repeat from * to end—154 (175, 196) sts. Knit 3 rnds.

Next Rnd: Change to 1x1 Rib; work even for 1 rnd. BO all sts in pattern.

bell sleeve blouse

SIZES
X-Small (Small, Medium, Large, X-Large, 2X-Large)

FINISHED MEASUREMENTS
32 (35, 38, 41, 44, 47)" bust

YARN
Aunt Lydia's Classic Crochet Thread (100% cotton; 350 yards / 50 grams): 5 (5, 6, 7, 7, 8) balls #131 Fudge Brown

NEEDLES
One 24" (60 cm) long circular (circ) needle size US 3 (3.25 mm)

One pair straight needles size US 7 (4.5 mm)

Change needle size if necessary to obtain correct gauge.

NOTIONS
Crochet hook size US D/3 (3.25 mm); stitch markers; stitch holder

GAUGE
24 sts and 32 rows = 4" (10 cm) in Stockinette stitch (St st), using smaller needle and 2 strands of yarn held together

20 sts and 22 rows = 4" (10 cm) in Lace Pattern from Chart, using larger needles and 2 strands of yarn held together

BODY

Using circ needle and 2 strands of yarn held together, CO 186 (204, 222, 240, 258, 276) sts. Join for working in the rnd; pm for beginning of rnd. Begin St st; work even for 7 rnds. Place right side marker after 93 (102, 111, 120, 129, 138) sts.

Shape Waist

Decrease Rnd: Decrease 4 sts this rnd, then every 8 rnds 5 times, as follows: [K2tog, knit to 2 sts before marker, ssk] twice—162 (180, 198, 216, 234, 252) sts remain. Work even until piece measures 7 1/2 (8, 8, 8 1/2, 8 1/2, 9)" from the beginning. Place bust markers after st 26 (29, 32, 35, 38, 41) and st 55 (61, 67, 73, 79, 85).

Shape Bust

Increase Rnd 1: Knit to bust marker, remove marker, [k1, p1, k1] in next st, reposition marker to after first k1, knit to 1 st before next marker, [k1, p1, k1] in next st, reposition marker to before second k1, knit to side marker, slip marker (sm), k1-f/b, knit to last st, k1-f/b—168 (186, 204, 222, 240, 258) sts. Work even for 5 rnds.

Increase Rnd 2: Knit to bust marker, remove marker, [k1, p1, k1] in next st, reposition marker to after first k1, knit to 1 st before next marker, [k1, p1, k1] in next st, reposition marker to before second k1, knit to end—172 (190, 208, 226, 244, 262) sts. Work even for 5 rnds.

Repeat last 12 rnds twice—192 (210, 228, 246, 264, 282) sts [105 (114, 123, 132, 141, 150) sts for Front; 87 (96, 105, 114, 123, 132) sts for Back]. Work even until piece measures 13 1/2 (14, 14 1/2, 15, 15 1/2, 16)" from the beginning, ending 4 (4, 5, 5, 6, 6) sts before end of last rnd.

BACK

Divide Front and Back: BO next 10 (10, 12, 12, 14, 14) sts, work to 6 (6, 7, 7, 8, 8) sts before side marker, place 93 (102, 109, 118, 125, 134) sts on holder for Front, BO next 10 (10, 12, 12, 14, 14) sts, work to end. Working only on remaining 79 (88, 95, 104, 111, 120) sts for Back, work even for 1 row.

Shape Armholes (RS): BO 2 sts at beginning of next 0 (2, 2, 4, 6, 8) rows, then decrease 1 st each side every other row 6 (7, 7, 8, 7, 8) times, as follows: K1, ssk, work to last 3 sts, k2tog, k1—67 (70, 77, 80, 85, 88) sts remain. Work even until armhole measures 5 (5 1/2, 6, 6 1/2, 7, 7 1/2)", ending with a WS row.

Shape Neck (RS): K21 (22, 24, 25, 26, 27), join a second ball of yarn, BO center 25 (26, 29, 30, 33, 34) sts, work to end. Working both sides at the same time, decrease 1 st each neck edge every other row 3 times— 18 (19, 21, 22, 23, 24) sts remain each side for shoulders. Work even until armhole measures 7 (7 1/2, 8, 8 1/2, 9, 9 1/2)" from the beginning, ending with a WS row.

Shape Shoulders (RS): BO 6 (6, 7, 7, 8, 8) sts at beginning of next 4 rows, then 6 (7, 7, 8, 7, 8) sts at beginning of next 2 rows.

New leaf motifs (framed Reverse Stockinette stitch and then Trellis Leaves) are created by working several times into a single stitch. The effect is a pod-shaped decorative hole, similar to an embroidered eyelet.

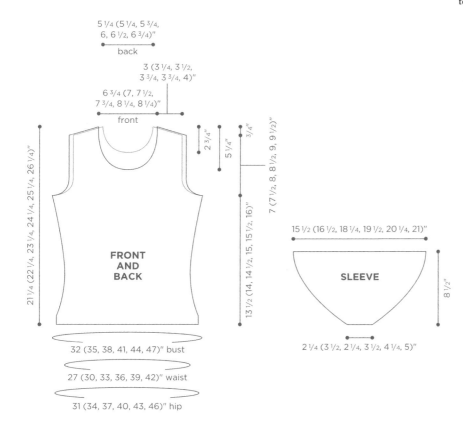

5 1/4 (5 1/4, 5 3/4, 6, 6 1/2, 6 3/4)"
back

3 (3 1/4, 3 1/2, 3 3/4, 3 3/4, 4)"

6 3/4 (7, 7 1/2, 7 3/4, 8 1/4, 8 1/4)"
front

2 3/4"

5 1/4"

3/4"

7 (7 1/2, 8, 8 1/2, 9, 9 1/2)"

21 1/4 (22 1/4, 23 1/4, 24 1/4, 25 1/4, 26 1/4)"

13 1/2 (14, 14 1/2, 15, 15 1/2, 16)"

FRONT AND BACK

32 (35, 38, 41, 44, 47)" bust

27 (30, 33, 36, 39, 42)" waist

31 (34, 37, 40, 43, 46)" hip

15 1/2 (16 1/2, 18 1/4, 19 1/2, 20 1/4, 21)"

SLEEVE

8 1/2"

2 1/4 (3 1/2, 2 1/4, 3 1/2, 4 1/4, 5)"

FRONT

With WS facing, rejoin yarn to sts on holder for Front. Purl 1 row.

Shape Armholes (RS): BO 2 sts at beginning of next 0 (2, 2, 4, 6, 8) rows, then decrease 1 st each side every other row 8 (9, 9, 10, 9, 10) times—77 (80, 87, 90, 95, 98) sts remain. Work even until armhole measures 2 ½ (3, 3 ½, 4, 4 ½, 5)", ending with a WS row.

Shape Neck (RS): K26 (27, 29, 30, 31, 32), join a second ball of yarn, BO center 25 (26, 29, 30, 33, 34) sts, work to end. Working both sides at the same, time, decrease 1 st each neck edge every row twice, every other row 4 times, then every 4 rows twice, and AT THE SAME TIME, when armhole measures same as for Back to shoulder shaping, shape shoulder as for Back.

SLEEVES

Note: Sleeves are worked from the top down.

Using larger needles and 2 strands of yarn held together, CO 11 (17, 11, 17, 21, 25) sts. Purl 1 row.

SIZES X-SMALL AND MEDIUM ONLY (RS): K1, work across 9 sts of Lace Pattern from Chart, k1.

SIZES SMALL AND LARGE ONLY (RS): K1, yo, ssk, k1, pm, work across 9 sts of Lace Pattern from Chart, pm, k1, yo, k2tog, k1.

SIZE X-LARGE ONLY (RS): K1, [yo, ssk] twice, k1, pm, work across 9 sts of Lace Pattern from Chart, pm, k1, [yo, k2tog] twice, k1.

SIZE 2X-LARGE ONLY (RS): K1, [yo, ssk] 3 times, k1, pm, work across 9 sts of Lace Pattern from Chart, pm, k1, [yo, k2tog] 3 times, k1.

LACE PATTERN

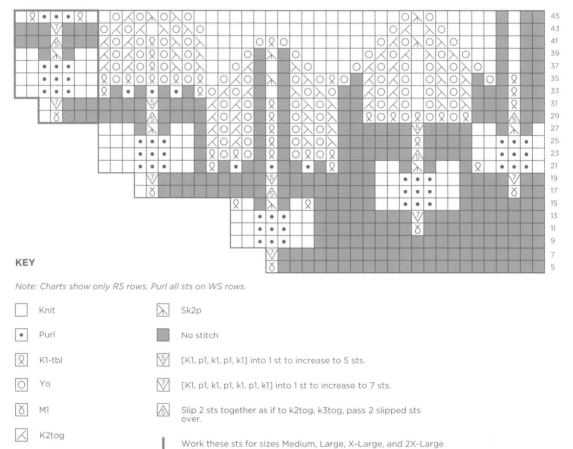

KEY

Note: Charts show only RS rows. Purl all sts on WS rows.

	Knit			Sk2p
•	Purl			No stitch
Ⴒ	K1-tbl	▽5	[K1, p1, k1, p1, k1] into 1 st to increase to 5 sts.
O	Yo	▽7	[K1, p1, k1, p1, k1, p1, k1] into 1 st to increase to 7 sts.
8	M1	▲5	Slip 2 sts together as if to k2tog, k3tog, pass 2 slipped sts over.
↗	K2tog		
↘	Ssk	❙	Work these sts for sizes Medium, Large, X-Large, and 2X-Large only.

ALL SIZES: Work even until entire Chart is complete, ending with a WS row—77 (83, 91, 97, 101, 105) sts. BO all sts, but do not cut yarn.

Crochet Sleeve Edging: With RS facing, using crochet hook and 2 strands of yarn held together, work Crab Stitch Edging (see Special Techniques, page 155) along BO edge. Fasten off.

FINISHING

Block to measurements. Sew shoulder seams. *Note: The Back and Front neck widths are intended to be slightly different, so the shoulders of the two pieces will not meet when the pieces are laid flat. However, since the shoulders are the same width, you will be able to sew the shoulder seams evenly.* Sew in Sleeves, matching center of Sleeve CO edge to shoulder seam, and leaving underarm BO unsewn.

Crochet Body Edging: With RS facing, using crochet hook and 2 strands of yarn held together, work Crab Stitch Edging along CO edge of Body. Fasten off.

Crochet Neck Edging: With RS facing, using crochet hook and 2 strands of yarn held together, and beginning at left shoulder, work Crab Stitch Edging around neck shaping. Fasten off.

hug-me-tight cardigan

NOTE
The Cardigan is constructed of the Body Panel, the Sleeves, which are picked up from the cast-on and bound-off edges of the Body Panel, the Collar, which is picked up from the center portion of one side edge of the Body Panel, and the Waist/Bust Band, which is sewn to the remaining portion of the side edges of the Body Panel.

ABBREVIATIONS
Sc2tog: Single crochet 2 sts together.

BODY PANEL
Using smaller circ needle, CO 158 (158, 184, 184, 210) sts. Begin Lace Improv Sampler from Chart. Work Rows 1-82 three times, then Rows 0 (1-18, 1-34, 1-50, 1-66) once (piece should measure approximately 26 (28, 29 1/2, 31, 33)" from the beginning. Block piece to measurements. Fold Panel in half lengthwise and place marker at fold along one side edge of Panel; place markers 4 (4 1/2, 5, 5 3/4, 6 1/4)" to either side of this marker, for Collar. Unfold Panel and now fold in half widthwise, so that side edges are together. Place markers 3 (2 1/2, 2 1/2, 2 1/2, 2)" in from CO

SIZES
X-Small (Small, Medium, Large, X-Large)

To fit bust sizes 32-34 (36-38, 40-42, 44-46, 48-50)". To select the size to work, measure from center front, beginning 5" down from breastbone, around to small of back, and up to the beginning point in order to get closest "hug" measurement.

FINISHED MEASUREMENTS
44 (46, 47 1/2, 49, 51)" cuff to cuff

YARN
Malabrigo Sock (100% superwash merino wool; 440 yards / 100 grams): 4 (4, 5, 5, 6) hanks #807 Côte d'Azure

NEEDLES
One 24" (60 cm) long or longer circular (circ) needle size US 3 (3.25 mm)

One 24" (60 cm) long circular needle size US 4 (3.5 mm)

One pair straight needles size US 4 (3.5 mm)

One set of five double-pointed needles (dpn) size US 4 (3.5 mm)

One set of five double-pointed needles size US 3 (3.25 mm)

Change needle size if necessary to obtain correct gauge.

NOTIONS
Crochet hook size US B/2 (2.75 mm); stitch markers; two 3/8" dome-shaped metal shank buttons

GAUGE
26 sts and 38 rows = 4" (10 cm) in Lace Improv Sampler from Chart, using smaller needle

30 sts and 37 rows = 4" (10 cm) in Eyelet Rib, using larger needles, slightly stretched

35 sts and 41 rows = 4" (10 cm) in Eyelet Rib, using smaller needle, slightly stretched

and BO edges along both side edges. Sew side edges together from BO or CO edge to markers, leaving center unsewn. With sewn edges facing away from you, and fold closest to you, and with side edge that is marked for Collar underneath the unmarked side edge, place markers for Sleeves halfway between seam and fold line along CO and BO edges of Body Panel (see schematic).

SLEEVES

Using larger dpns, beginning and ending at marker, pick up and knit 95 (95, 115, 115, 125) sts along CO edge of Body Panel. Join for working in the rnd; place marker (pm) for beginning of rnd.

Eyelet Rib

Rnds 1, 2, 3, and 5: *K3, p2; repeat from * to end.

Rnd 4: *K3, yo, p2tog; repeat from * to end.

Rnd 6: Repeat Rnd 1.

Repeat Rnds 1-6 until piece measures 1" from pick-up rnd. Change to smaller dpns; work even until piece measures 3" from pick-up rnd, ending with Rnd 6 of Eyelet Rib.

For the Lace Improv pattern repeat, I combined small motifs from several Art Deco doilies—pine tree, diamonds, stylized double eyelet flower—for a visual representation of the Jazz Age.

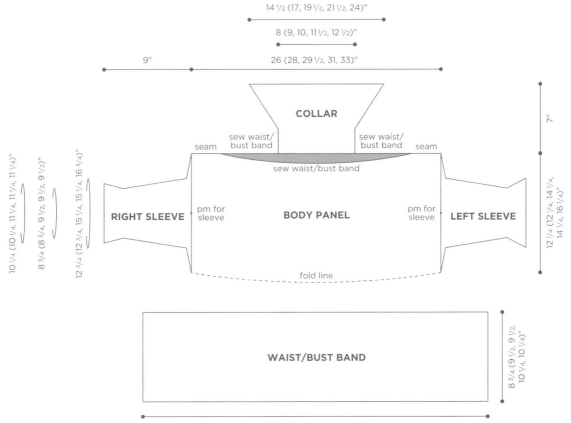

14 1/2 (17, 19 1/2, 21 1/2, 24)"

8 (9, 10, 11 1/2, 12 1/2)"

9"

26 (28, 29 1/2, 31, 33)"

COLLAR

7"

seam

sew waist/ bust band

sew waist/ bust band

seam

sew waist/bust band

10 1/4 (10 1/4, 11 1/4, 11 1/4, 11 1/4)"

8 3/4 (8 3/4, 9 1/2, 9 1/2, 9 1/2)"

12 3/4 (12 3/4, 15 1/4, 15 1/4, 16 3/4)"

12 1/4 (12 3/4, 14 1/4, 14 1/4, 16 1/4)"

RIGHT SLEEVE

pm for sleeve

BODY PANEL

pm for sleeve

LEFT SLEEVE

fold line

WAIST/BUST BAND

8 3/4 (9 1/2, 9 1/2, 10 1/4, 10 1/4)"

36 (40, 42, 43 1/2, 47 1/2)"

LACE IMPROV SAMPLER

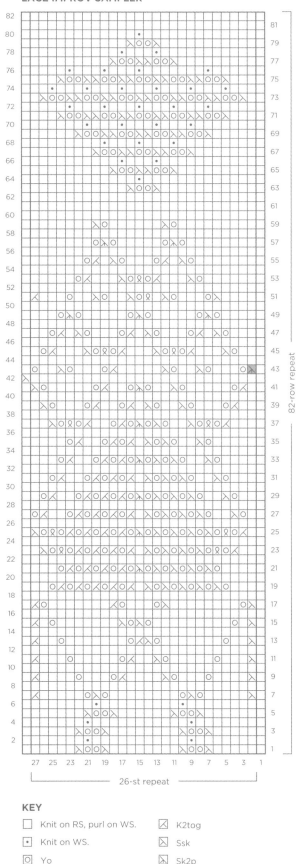

KEY

☐	Knit on RS, purl on WS.	⟋	K2tog
•	Knit on WS.	⟍	Ssk
O	Yo	⋏	Sk2p
ℓ	K1-tbl	▨	Work as k2tog on first repeat only; work as sk2p on subsequent repeats.

Dec Rnd: Decrease 1 st each repeat, as follows: *K2tog, k1, p2; repeat from * to end—76 (76, 92, 92, 100) sts remain. Work even for 1 rnd.

SIZES MEDIUM, LARGE, AND X-LARGE ONLY

Shape Sleeve: Continuing in Eyelet Rib as established, decrease 2 sts this rnd, then every (—, 6, 6, 4) rnds (—, 3, 3, 7) times, as follows: Ssk, work to last 2 sts, k2tog—(—, 84, 84, 84) sts remain.

ALL SIZES: Work even until piece measures 7" from pick-up rnd. Change to larger dpns. Work even until piece measures 9" from pick-up rnd. BO all sts in pattern. Repeat for opposite Sleeve.

WAIST/BUST BAND

Using larger straight needles, CO 66 (71, 71, 76, 76) sts.

Eyelet Rib

Row 1 (RS): *P3, k2; repeat from * to last 6 sts, [p1, k1] 3 times.

Rows 2, 3, and 5: Knit the knit sts and purl the purl sts as they face you.

Row 4: [P1, k1] 3 times, *yo, p2tog, k3; repeat from * to end.

Row 6: Knit the knit sts and purl the purl sts as they face you; knit all yos.

Repeat Rows 1-6 until piece measures approximately 36 (40, 42, 43 1/2, 47 1/2)" from the beginning, ending with Row 6 of Eyelet Rib. BO all sts in pattern.

COLLAR

With RS of Body Panel facing, using smaller circ needle, pick up and knit 69 (79, 89, 99, 109) sts between Collar markers.

Eyelet Rib

Row 1 (WS): [K1, p1] 3 times, k2, *p3, k2; repeat from * to last 6 sts, [p1, k1] 3 times.

Rows 2, 3, and 5: Knit the knit sts and purl the purl sts as they face you.

Row 4: [P1, k1] 3 times, yo, p2tog, *k3, yo, p2tog; repeat from * to last 6 sts, [k1, p1] 3 times.

Row 6: Knit the knit sts and purl the purl sts as they face you; knit all yos.

Repeat Rows 1-6 until piece measures approximately 3″ from pick-up row, ending with Row 6 of Eyelet Rib.

Reverse Eyelet Rib

Row 1 (WS): [K1, p1] 3 times, p2, *k3, p2; repeat from * to last 6 sts, [p1, k1] 3 times.

Rows 2-4: Knit the knit sts and purl the purl sts as they face you.

Row 5 (Increase Row): [K1, p1] 3 times, yo, p2tog, yo, *k3, yo, p2tog, yo; repeat from * to last 6 sts, [p1, k1] 3 times—81 (93, 105, 117, 129) sts.

Rows 6-10: Knit the knit sts and purl the purl sts as they face you; knit all yos.

Row 11: [K1, p1] 3 times, yo, p3tog, yo, *k3, yo, p3tog, yo; repeat from * to last 6 sts, [p1, k1] 3 times.

Rows 12-16: Repeat Row 6.

Row 17 (Increase Row): Change to larger circ needle. [K1, p1] 3 times, yo, p2tog, p1, yo, *k3, yo, p2tog, p1, yo; repeat from * to last 6 sts, [p1, k1] 3 times—93 (107, 121, 135, 149) sts.

Rows 18-22: Repeat Row 6.

Row 23 (Increase Row): [K1, p1] 3 times, yo, p1, p2tog, p1, yo, *k3, yo, p1, p2tog, p1, yo; repeat from * to last 6 sts, [p1, k1] 3 times—105 (121, 137, 153, 169) sts.

Rows 24-28: Repeat Row 6.

Row 29: [K1, p1] 3 times, yo, p2tog, p1, p2tog, yo, *k3, yo, p2tog, p1, p2tog, yo; repeat from * to last 6 sts, [p1, k1] 3 times.

Rows 30-34: Repeat Row 6.

Row 35 (Increase Row): [K1, p1] 3 times, yo, p2tog, yo, p1, yo, p2tog, yo, *k3, yo, p2tog, yo, p1, yo, p2tog, yo; repeat from * to last 6 sts, [p1, k1] 3 times—129 (149, 169, 189, 209) sts.

Rows 36-40: Repeat Row 6.

Row 41: [K1, p1] 3 times, [yo, p2tog] 3 times, *yo, k2tog, k1, ssk, yo, p2tog, yo, p1, yo, p2tog; repeat from * to last 17 sts, yo, k2tog, k1, ssk, yo, [p2tog, yo] 3 times, [p1, k1] 3 times.

Rows 42-46: Repeat Row 6.

FINISHING

With RS of Body Panel and Waist/Bust Band facing, sew left-hand (p3) edge of Waist/Bust Band to open edges of Body Panel, beginning and ending on either side of Collar. Sew approximately 2 1/2″ of side edges of Collar to CO and BO edges of Waist/Bust Band.

Covered Buttons (optional): Using crochet hook, chain 4 and join with slip st to first chain to form a loop.

Rnd 1: Work 8 sc into loop.

Rnd 2: Sc twice into each st—16 sts.

Rnd 3: Sc once into each st.

Rnd 4: *Sc into 1 st, sc twice into next st; repeat from * to end—24 sts.

Rnd 5: Repeat Rnd 4—36 sts.

Rnds 6-8: Sc. Insert button into cover.

Rnd 9: *Sc, sc2tog; repeat from * to end—24 sts remain.

Rnd 10: Repeat Rnd 9—16 sts.

Rnd 11: *Sc2tog; repeat from * to end—8 sts remain. Fasten off and cut yarn, leaving long tail. Thread tail through sts of last rnd and pull tight to close hole around shank of button.

Sew buttons to left edge of Waist/Bust Band, 4 sts in from edge, the first button 1″ below CO edge of Waist/Bust Band, and the second 2 1/4″ below the first. Buttons will button through eyelets on opposite edge of Waist/Bust Band.

palm leaf wrap

FINISHED MEASUREMENTS

35 (41½, 48)" along CO edge, not including fringe

YARN

O-Wool Legacy Bulky (100% certified organic merino wool; 106 yards / 100 grams): 4 (5, 6) hanks #3212 Sprig

NEEDLES

One 29" (70 cm) long or longer circular (circ) needle size US 13 (9 mm)

Change needle size if necessary to obtain correct gauge.

GAUGE

10 sts and 13 rows = 4" (10 cm) in Stockinette stitch (St st)

NOTES

To make it easier to work the charts for this pattern, the Wrap is worked with the right side facing at all times. After each Chart row is complete, you will slide the stitches to the opposite end of the needle to work the next row, pulling out a 20" length of yarn before beginning the row.

When working the first stitch of the next row, you will leave the 20" length of yarn hanging free. Once the chart is complete, you will have one loop for each row worked. These loops will be cut in the center to form the fringe.

ABBREVIATIONS

Pso: pass next-to-last st on right-hand needle over last st and off needle.

WRAP

Using Long-Tail CO (see Special Techniques, page 154), CO 123 (146, 169) sts. Do not turn; slide sts back to right-hand end of needle. Leave a length of yarn 20" long (or twice the desired length of the fringe). Begin Palm Leaf Pattern from Chart; work even until entire Chart is complete, working each row on the RS, sliding sts to right-hand end of needle after each row is complete, and leaving 20" length of yarn at end of each Chart row—238 (284, 330) sts remain after entire Chart is complete.

BO Row (RS): *BO 7 sts, slip st from right-hand needle back to left-hand needle, k2tog, k5, turn, p6, turn, BO 5 sts, k1 into 2 sts below next st on left-hand needle (the next st on left-hand needle is a k2tog, so you knit into the 2 sts that were knit together on the previous rnd) letting st drop from left-hand needle, pso, [slip st from right-hand needle back to left-hand needle, k2tog, k6, turn, p7, turn, BO 6 sts, k1 into 2 sts below next st on left-hand needle dropping st from left-hand needle, pso] 4 times; repeat from * to last 7 sts, BO to end.

FINISHING

Cut each loose 20" strand of yarn at center to form fringe. Tie strands together in pairs at edge to secure. Trim fringe if necessary. Block as desired. The CO edge forms an upside-down vee at the center of each leaf. To draw in neck edge and create a capelet fit, sew every other leaf along the sides of the vee and keep the remaining vees unsewn. Or to create a shaped poncho fit, fold CO edge in half, and sew interlocking vees together, leaving center open for neck.

This every-row lace pattern forces the diagonal openwork into an extreme slant, making it look horizontal. The stitches of the Leaf Insert chart appear almost perpendicular to the stitches of the Palm Leaf Pattern chart.

PALM LEAF PATTERN

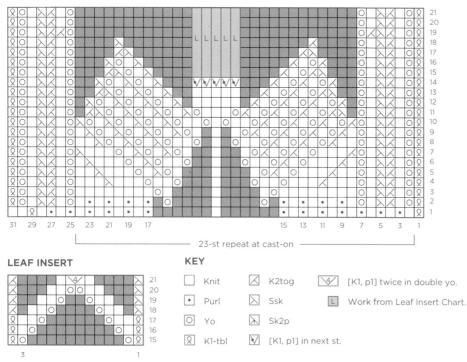

23-st repeat at cast-on

LEAF INSERT

KEY

	Knit		K2tog		[K1, p1] twice in double yo.
•	Purl		Ssk	L	Work from Leaf Insert Chart.
O	Yo		Sk2p		
	K1-tbl		[K1, p1] in next st.		

Casting On

LONG-TAIL (THUMB) CO
Leaving tail with about 1" of yarn for each st to be CO, make a slipknot in the yarn and place it on the right-hand needle, with the tail to the front and the working end to the back. Insert the thumb and forefinger of your left hand between the strands of yarn so that the working end is around your forefinger, and the tail end is around your thumb "slingshot" fashion; *insert the tip of the right-hand needle into the front loop on the thumb, hook the strand of yarn coming from the forefinger from back to front, and draw it through the loop on your thumb; remove your thumb from the loop and pull on the working yarn to tighten the new st on the right-hand needle; return your thumb and forefinger to their original positions, and repeat from * for remaining sts to be CO.

PROVISIONAL CO
Using waste yarn, CO the required number of sts; work in Stockinette st for 3 or 4 rows; work 1 row with a thin, smooth yarn (crochet cotton or ravel cord used for machine knitting) as a separator; change to main yarn and continue as directed. When ready to work the live sts, pull out the separator row, placing the live sts on a spare needle.

Shaping

SHAPING WITHIN LACE
When not specified in the pattern, individual knitters must use their own judgment to shape armholes, necklines, and other areas. Consideration should be given to the yarn gauge and strength, and to whether the edge will have a seam or other finishing. For instance, when a garment has a very sheer lace pattern, it may look clumsy to forego the yos closest to the shaped edge as that would create a more solid area (especially in a heavier gauge). But, at the same time, too many yos worked too close to the shaped edge without solid sts may be overly frail and awkward to seam.

Basically, when working decreases at an edge, it is necessary to maintain the lace pattern as much as possible without losing st count. And you will need to keep the st pattern oriented correctly; placing st markers between repeats across a piece provides a visual reference as the margins of a piece change—just count back from the nearest full repeat. Here is an easy option: If the st pattern has a plain WS row, I recommend working the decreases (if they are to be worked every other row or every 4 rows) on WS rows.

When working a standard decrease on a lace row, there must be enough sts to work a decrease for every yo in the st pattern, plus accommodate the 2 edge sts (or 3 with selvage) necessary for the shaping decrease. The advantage of using this standard method is strong shaping lines along either edge that provide a visual cue while working and are easy to align, plus they can be a design element (on raglans and necklines you can choose outward or inward slanting decreases to complement the st pattern). In addition, there are many decorative decreases that include a yo and extra decrease to create striking faggoting detail.

Here is another shaping method to use when you have few sts to work with at the edge: Instead of dedicating separate sts to the shaping decrease, work the nearest decrease that appears in the st pattern, but do not work the corresponding yo next to it. When worked in the appropriate area of the st pattern—for instance, along the edge of a diamond that has a slanted decrease—this method can make the shaping area appear organic to the pattern motif.

Increasing is often built into the lace pattern or worked with yos in order to enhance the lace. When you wish to maintain the yo edge but no longer increase, you might work a yo paired with a decrease. Sleeves worked in lace from the cuff can present more of a challenge—as increasing creates new sts, you need to decide when there are enough to work them into the st pattern. You might use st markers to delineate the pattern repeats nearest to the edge, then work portions of the pattern from the chart when you have enough sts to work a decrease with its paired increase, keeping in mind that sometimes the increase and decrease are separated by a number of sts.

SHORT ROW SHAPING
Work the number of sts specified in the instructions, wrap and turn (wrp-t) as follows:

To wrap a knit st, bring yarn to the front (purl position), slip the next st purlwise to the right-hand needle, bring yarn to the back of work, return the slipped st on the right-hand needle to the left-hand needle purlwise; turn, ready to work the next row, leaving the remaining sts unworked. To wrap a purl st, work as for wrapping a knit st, but bring yarn to the back (knit position) before slipping the stitch, and to the front after slipping the stitch.

When short rows are completed, or when working progressively longer short rows, work the wrap together with the wrapped st as you come to it as follows:

If st is to be worked as a knit st, insert the right-hand needle into the wrap, from below, then into the wrapped st; k2tog; if st to be worked is a purl st, insert needle into the wrapped st, then down into the wrap; p2tog. (It may be easier to lift wrap onto the left-hand needle, then work it together with the wrapped st.)

Charts

READING CHARTS

Unless otherwise specified in the instructions, when working straight, charts are read from right to left for RS rows, from left to right for WS rows. Row numbers are written at the beginning of each row. Numbers on the right indicate RS rows; numbers on the left indicate WS rows. When working circular, all rounds are read from right to left.

NO STITCH

Because the st count sometimes varies when working lace, charts often utilize a "no stitch" box as a sort of placeholder to keep a space for a st that either will appear in a later row or has been decreased from a previous row. This method helps to visually represent particular st groupings and to center and align the chart pattern rows to look more like the work on the needles. Without employing "no stitch" boxes, some charts would have ragged edges and be hard to count and interpret. Here is an example of a pattern charted with and without "no stitch" boxes.

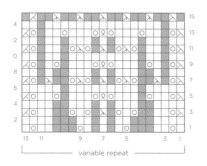

variable repeat

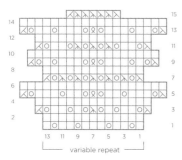

variable repeat

STITCH COUNT

When working from a lace chart, you may find the difference in st count from one chart row to the next confusing. Sometimes you won't work the same number of increases as decreases, causing the st count to change. The chart shows what the sts will look like when each row is complete. To verify the number of sts needed to work a given chart row, count the sts in that row, omitting all "no stitch" boxes and yarnovers, and making sure to count all the sts involved in each decrease (for instance, count a k2tog as 2 sts, or an s2kp as 3 sts). This is the number of sts you will need to work this row. Next count the same row, again omitting any "no stitch" boxes, but now counting all yarnovers, and making sure to count each decrease as the number of sts that are left after working the decrease (for instance, count a k2tog or s2kp as 1 st). This is the number of sts that you will have after working this row, and the number you will need to work the following row. If this is not the number of sts you have left after working the row (allowing for repeats and any edge sts worked outside the chart), double check to make sure that you worked the row correctly.

Finishing

CRAB STITCH EDGING

Row 1 (Single Crochet): Work from right to left for right-handers, or from left to right for left-handers. Make a slipknot and place on hook. *Insert hook into next st (along lower or upper edge) or between two rows (side edges). Yo hook, pull through to RS—2 loops on hook. Yo hook, draw through both loops—1 loop on hook. Repeat from * to end. *Note: It may be necessary to skip a row every so often when working along a side edge, in order to prevent puckering.*

Row 2 (Reverse Single Crochet): Work from left to right for right-handers, or from right to left for left-handers. *Insert hook into previous single crochet, yo hook, pull through to RS—2 loops on hook. Yo hook, draw through both loops—1 loop on hook. Repeat from * to end. Fasten off.

CROCHET CHAIN

Make a slipknot and place it on crochet hook. Holding tail end of yarn in left hand, *take hook under ball end of yarn from front to back; draw yarn on hook back through previous st on hook to form new st. Repeat from * to desired number of sts or length of chain.

KITCHENER STITCH

Using a blunt tapestry needle, thread a length of yarn approximately 4 times the length of the section to be joined. Hold the pieces to be joined wrong sides together, with the needles holding the sts parallel, both ends pointing to the right. Working from right to left, insert tapestry needle into first st on front needle as if to purl, pull yarn through, leaving st on needle; insert tapestry needle into first st on back needle as if to knit, pull yarn through, leaving st on needle; *insert tapestry needle into first st on front needle as if to knit, pull yarn through, remove st from needle; insert tapestry needle into next st on front needle as if to purl, pull yarn through, leave st on needle; insert tapestry needle into first st on back needle as if to purl, pull yarn through, remove st from needle; insert tapestry needle into next st on back needle as if to knit, pull yarn through, leave st on needle. Repeat from *, working 3 or 4 sts at a time, then go back and adjust tension to match the pieces being joined. When 1 st remains on each needle, cut yarn and pass through last 2 sts to fasten off.

BO = Bind off

Circ = Circular

Cn = Cable needle

CO = Cast on

Dpn = Double-pointed needle(s)

K1-f/b = Knit into the front loop and back loop of the same stitch to increase 1 stitch.

K1-tbl = Knit 1 stitch through the back loop.

K2tog = Knit 2 stitches together.

K3tog = Knit 3 stitches together.

K4tog = Knit 4 stitches together.

K = Knit

M1 or M1-l (make 1 left slanting) = With the tip of the left-hand needle inserted from front to back, lift the strand between the 2 needles onto the left-hand needle; knit the strand through the back loop to increase 1 stitch.

M1-r (make 1 right slanting) = With the tip of the left-hand needle inserted from back to front, lift the strand between the 2 needles onto the left-hand needle; knit the strand through the front loop to increase 1 stitch.

P2tog = Purl 2 stitches together.

Pm = Place marker

P = Purl

Psso (pass slipped stitch over) = Pass the slipped stitch on the right-hand needle over the stitch(es) indicated in the instructions, as in binding off.

Rnd(s) = Round(s)

RS = Right side

S2kp2 = Slip the next 2 stitches together to the right-hand needle as if to knit 2 together, k1, pass the 2 slipped stitches over.

Sc (single crochet) = Insert the hook into the next stitch and draw up a loop (2 loops on the hook), yarn over and draw through both loops on the hook.

Sk2p (double decrease) = Slip the next stitch knitwise to the right-hand needle, k2tog, pass the slipped stitch over the stitch from the k2tog.

Sm = Slip marker

Ssk (slip, slip, knit) = Slip the next 2 stitches to the right-hand needle one at a time as if to knit; return them to the left-hand needle one at a time in their new orientation; knit them together through the back loops.

Sssk = Same as ssk, but worked on the next 3 stitches.

St(s) = Stitch(es)

Tbl = Through the back loop

Tog = Together

WS = Wrong side

Wrp-t = Wrap and turn (see Special Techniques—Short Row Shaping)

Yb = Yarn back

Yf = Yarn front

Yo = When the next stitch is to be knit, bring the yarn to the front, then knit the next stitch; this will take the yarn over the needle to the back as you knit. When the next stitch is to be purled, bring the yarn over the top of the needle to the back, then to the front again, ready to purl the next stitch.

Yo twice = When 2 yarnover symbols appear next to each other in a chart, work a yo twice around the needle, ending with the yarn in back if the next stitch is to be knit or with the yarn in front if the next stitch is to be purled. On the following row, work each of the 2 yarnover wraps as separate stitches, unless otherwise indicated.

Yrn = Bring the yarn over the top of the needle to the front, then to the back again, ready to knit the next stitch.

Work even = Continue working in the pattern or patterns as established. Note that if the stitch pattern includes any shaping *within* the pattern (as opposed to shaping along an armhole or neck edge), such as for the Smocked Border Triangle Shawl (page 74), you will continue to work the shaping within the pattern.

RESOURCES

To locate the retailer of a specific yarn used for a project, contact the manufacturer/distributor listed below. The company or a yarn shop can help you to make a substitution for any discontinued yarn based on the yarn weight, structure, and fiber content provided in the instructions. The website www.yarndex.com can also be very helpful for making substitutions.

Alchemy Yarns of Transformation
PO Box 1080
Sebastopol, CA 95473
707.823.3276
www.alchemyyarns.com

Artyarns
39 Westmoreland Avenue
White Plains, NY 10606
914.428.0333
www.artyarns.com

Blue Sky Alpacas, Inc.
PO Box 88
Cedar, MN 55011
763.753.5815
www.blueskyalpacas.com

Cascade
1224 Andover Park East
Tukwila, WA 98188
800.548.1048
www.cascadeyarns.com

Crystal Palace Yarns/Straw into Gold, Inc.
160 23rd Street
Richmond, CA 94804
800.666.7455
www.straw.com

DMC Corporation
10 Basin Drive, Suite 130
Kearny, NJ 07032
973.589.0606
www.dmc-usa.com

Filatura Di Crosa, distributed by Tahki • Stacy Charles, Inc.

Jamieson's of Shetland
Sandness Industrial Estate
Sandness Shetland
ZE2 9PL
www.jamiesonsshetland.co.uk.

Lanaknits Hemp For Knitting
Suite 3B, 320 Vernon Street
Nelson, BC, V1L 4E4, Canada
888.301.0011
www.hempforknitting.com

LB Studio, Lion Brand Yarn
135 Kero Road
Carlstadt, NJ 07072
800.258.YARN
www.lionbrand.com

Loop-d-Loop by Teva Durham, distributed by Tahki • Stacy Charles, Inc.

Lorna's Laces
4229 North Honore Street
Chicago, IL 60613
773.935.3803
www.lornaslaces.net

Louet North America
3425 Hands Road
Prescott, ON, K0E 1T0, Canada
800.897.6444
www.louet.com

Malabrigo Yarn
Miami, FL
786.866.6187
www.malabrigoyarn.com

O-Wool
Tunney Wool Company
915 N. 28th Street
Philadelphia, PA 19130
888.673.0260
www.tunneywoolcompany.com

Rowan
Westminster Fibers, Inc.
165 Ledge Street
Nashua, NH 03060
800.445.9276
www.westminsterfibers.com

Tahki, distributed by Tahki • Stacy Charles, Inc.

Tahki • Stacy Charles, Inc.
70-30 80th Street, Building 36
Ridgewood, NY 11385
800.338.YARN
www.tahkistacycharles.com

Dakota Trimming (Notions)
251 West 39th Street
New York, NY 10018
212.354.1713

Sunbelt Fastener Co. (12″ wooden purse handle SFPH-W03-N)
8841 Exposition Boulevard
Culver City, CA 90230
800.642.6587
www.sunbeltfastener.com

ADDITIONAL RESOURCES AND REFERENCES

INTERNET RESOURCES

www.eunnyjang.com/knit/2006/03/majoring_in_lace_introduction_1.html
Before taking the helm of Interweave Knits, Eunny Jang wrote this excellent tutorial on lace, which is still archived and well worth visiting.

www.islandofmisfitpatterns.com/2006/07/28/fix-a-missing-yarn-over/
A helpful technique with photographs of how to fix a missed yarnover from the row above.

www.knittingbeyondthehebrides.org
An excellent online lace symposium with interviews and instruction contributed by many excellent lace knitters.

www.laceknitter.blogspot.com
A fascinating project undertaken by a blogger in possession of an 1884 sampler book to translate the patterns into charts.

www.thewalkertreasury.wordpress.com
A cooperative project in which knitters are posting clear color swatches knit from Barbara Walker's stitch dictionaries (does not include stitch instructions).

www.vam.ac.uk/collections/fashion/features/knitting/index.html
The website of the Victoria and Albert Museum in London with images of knit artifacts and a good array of knitting links.

www.victorian-embroidery-and-crafts.com
Historical information and some free authentic Victorian knitting patterns.

www.wonderhowto.com/how-to-use-lifeline-4564/
A how-to video on inserting a "lifeline" so you can unravel back to a specific pattern row.

www.yarnover.net
Home of a lace knitting web ring with information and some stitch patterns.

PRINTED REFERENCES

Abbey, Barbara. *Barbara Abbey's Knitting Lace* (Schoolhouse Press, 1993); originally published in 1974 by The Viking Press.

Foley, Tricia. *Linens and Lace* (Clarkson Potter, 1990).

Kinzel, Marianne. *First Book of Modern Lace Knitting* (Dover Publications, Inc., 1972); originally published in 1954 by Artistic Needlework Publications, London.

Kinzel, Marianne. *Second Book of Modern Lace Knitting* (Dover Publications, Inc., 1972); originally published in 1961 by Mills & Boon Limited, London.

Korach, Alice. "Shetland Lace" in *Knitting Around The World from Threads* (Taunton Press, 1993).

Lewis, Susanna E. *Knitting Lace: A Workshop with Patterns and Projects* (Taunton Press, 1992).

Stanley, Montse. "Catalan Knit Lace" in *Knitting Around the World from Threads* (Taunton Press, 1993).

Starmore, Alice. "Unravelling The Myths of Shetland Lace" in *Knitting Around the World from Threads* (Taunton Press, 1993).

Thomas, Mary. *Mary Thomas's Book of Knitting Patterns* (Dover Publications, Inc., 1972); originally published in 1942 by Hodder and Stoughton, Ltd., London.

Walker, Barbara G. *A Treasury of Knitting Patterns* (Schoolhouse Press, 1998); originally published in 1968 by Charles Scribner's Sons.

Walker, Barbara G. *A Second Treasury of Knitting Patterns* (Schoolhouse Press, 1998); originally published in 1970 by Charles Scribner's Sons.

Walker, Barbara G. *Charted Knitting Designs: A Third Treasury of Knitting Patterns* (Schoolhouse Press, 1998); originally published in 1972 by Charles Scribner's Sons.

Walker, Barbara G. *A Fourth Treasury of Knitting Patterns* (Schoolhouse Press, 2001); originally published as *Sampler Knitting* in 1973 by Charles Scribner's Sons.

ACKNOWLEDGMENTS

LACE IS A METAPHOR FOR OUR lives—vulnerable yet strong, there is beauty in what is absent as well as in what is present; without the holes we could not see the pattern. I have become intimate with the metaphor of lace over the last several years. Soon after my second book came out, I embarked on this project and began to brainstorm how I could do something unexpected and unique with lace. It was an exciting and busy time; I had just started a signature yarn line and learned soon after that I was expecting my second child. Complications in the pregnancy delayed my progress and then my son was born with medical conditions and died at three months. I was heartbroken and lost passion for my work. Finishing this book has been one of my most challenging endeavors, but work has helped to heal my pain. I now look at cobweb Shetland shawls in a different way. Historians wonder that these magnificently complex Shetland shawls were created by "unsophisticated" islanders under dire circumstances, by sailor's widows in dirt huts. I do not wonder. I know that it is in the nature of humans to create and invent such extraordinary objects despite the limitations and trials of everyday life. This is perhaps our best quality.

All the people involved in producing this book have been patient with me and respectful of my work and have helped to make it shine. I have to thank Melanie Falick for her foresight in suggesting a lace book. I have learned so much from delving into this genre and it will forever affect my designing. My editor, Liana Allday, has been a positive and encouraging influence on the project. I am grateful to my agent, Caroline Greeven, for this book, and wish her the best in future endeavors. I am grateful to book designer, Anna Christian, who has continued with the striking format that she established with my first two books. Most importantly, I am indebted to technical editor Sue McCain who more than met the challenge of presenting sized garments with complex lace patterning with clear instructions and amazing charts.

Several wonderful knitters aided me in knitting and testing the patterns and without their assistance this book would not have been possible. They are: Jacqueline Chambers, Pat Chen, Papatya Curtis, Shelda Eggers, Kristin Frazier, Sandy Halpin, Lisa Hoffman, Margaux Pena Hufnagel, Irina Poludnenko, Jennifer Sonnenberg, Miriam Tegels, and Linda Wallis. They are from all across the country—New York, Tacoma, a core group in Missouri, California— and one, Miriam, from Holland. Several others helped in sewing linings, buttons, and zippers—Karina Feliz-Oropeza, Esther Mizrahhi, Jessamyn Leib, and my mother, Minerva Durham.

Photographer Adrian Buckmaster has once again given his special touch to my work and captured the beauty of the stitchwork. The book was shot in Adrian's studio in Bushwick, Brooklyn, where he treated us to lunches of his own homecooked celery/tomato pasta sauce, cilantro hummus, and other treats. We had a great team with whom we've worked on several projects now: stylist Kristen Petliski, makeup artist Deity Delgado, hair stylist Terri Graul, and photo assistant Allison Ugosoli. Our lovely models, Boyana, Ming, Heidi, Heather, Vienna, and Milo the cat, each added personality to the projects.

During the past several years I have been fortunate to work with a top yarn company, Tahki Stacy Charles, in creating my own yarn line. These yarns possess specific qualities that have allowed me to express my vision, and I've used them for several projects here. I have especially enjoyed the insight of industry leaders and company founders Stacy Charles and Diane Friedman. Debbi Skinner has offered great assistance and encouragement. In addition, several of my fellow knitting authors have helped me through tough times—this career would suck without the camaraderie of such talented colleagues. I am particularly grateful for the bonds developed along the way and the friendship of Kristeen Griffin-Grimes, Lynne Barr, Véronik Avery, Lela Nargi, Kari Cornell, Shannon Okey, and Dora Ohrenstein.

Teva Durham is the founder of loop-d-loop.com, a former editor at *Vogue Knitting International*, and the author of STC Craft's *Loop-d-Loop* (2005) and *Loop-d-Loop Crochet* (2007). Her designs and articles are featured in top knitting and crochet magazines and numerous books, including STC Craft's *Reversible Knitting* and *Weekend Knitting*. Her yarn and pattern line, called Loop-d-Loop, is distributed by Tahki Stacy Charles.

Adrian Buckmaster is a portrait, fashion, and landscape photographer who resides in Manhattan. He has worked extensively in New York and London for various magazines and is a member of the Art Workers Guild founded by William Morris.